The Wesleys and the
English Language

The Wesleys
AND
the English Language

FOUR ESSAYS

by

G. H. Vallins

WIPF & STOCK · Eugene, Oregon

Wipf and Stock Publishers
199 W 8th Ave, Suite 3
Eugene, OR 97401

The Wesleys and the English Language
Four Essays
By Vallins, G. H.
Copyright©1957 Methodist Publishing - Epworth Press
ISBN 13: 978-1-5326-4632-4
Publication date 12/28/2017
Previously published by Epworth Press, 1957

Every effort has been made to trace the current
copyright owner of this publication but without success.
If you have any information or interest in the copyright,
please contact the publishers.

Contents

1. JOHN WESLEY'S *GRAMMAR*   9

2. JOHN WESLEY'S *DICTIONARY*   26

3. THE SYNTAX OF JOHN WESLEY'S *JOURNAL* 50

4. THE LANGUAGE, METRE, AND RHYME
    OF CHARLES WESLEY'S HYMNS   69

The Wesleys and the English Language

I
John Wesley's *Grammar*

ON THURSDAY 11th December 1750 John Wesley 'prepared a short *History of England* for the use of children; and on Friday and Saturday a short *Roman History*, as an introduction to the Latin historians'. As if that was not enough, on the following Monday (15th December) he 'read over Mr Holmes's *Latin Grammar*, and extracted from it what was needful to perfect our own'. About two months later he was in London nursing a sprained ankle which he sustained on Sunday 10th February (1751) by slipping on the ice in the middle of London Bridge. He managed to preach at Snowfields (Seven Dials) in the morning, but, 'the sprain growing worse', he could not preach at the Foundery in the evening. So he 'removed to Threadneedle Street'; and there for the rest of the week he busied himself, outside his intervals of prayer and conversation, with 'writing an *Hebrew Grammar* and *Lessons for Children*'. To write five books (besides abridging others) in not much more than so many weeks is certainly a remarkable feat; but it is the kind of feat that —even without the enforced leisure arising from a sprained ankle—John Wesley all through his life made commonplace.

The background of all this educational activity was, of course, Kingswood School; though long before this, in Savannah during 1737, he had 'devoted his attention to Grammars, of which he more or less completed several before he left Savannah'. It was during that period of 1750-1 already referred to that he turned his thought to the needs of Kingswood. The first edition of the English

Grammar is dated 1753, the second, from which the quotations in this book are made, 1761. In the *Journal* for Friday 21st June 1751 he 'drew up a short account of the case of Kingswood School'. He mentions in it certain discouragements, and continues: 'Notwithstanding which, through God's help, I went on; wrote an English, a Latin, a Greek, a Hebrew, and a French Grammar, and printed *Praelectiones Pueriles*, with many other books for the use of the School.' It was a period of intense interest in the English language. Dryden had written on points of usage, maintaining, among other things, that a sentence should not end with a preposition. Early in the eighteenth century several *Spectator* papers by Addison and Steele had dealt with matters of speech and writing. The Royal Society had given its attention to the syntax and vocabulary of prose, and had encouraged the idea of the establishment of an Academy, on the lines of the Académie française, for what Swift called, in the title of a famous tract, *Correcting, Improving, and Ascertaining*[1] *the English Tongue*. There was a general belief among literary men that English was being corrupted by colloquialisms and abbreviations; and they were anxious to protect its purity and dignity. Language was 'in the air'—very much, in fact, as it is today.

The result was that the middle of the century witnessed the beginning of a spate of grammars and dictionaries. In the early seventeen-sixties two grammars appeared of outstanding importance—*The Rudiments of English Grammar* by the eminent scientist, Joseph Priestley, and *A Short Introduction to English Grammar* by Robert Lowth, afterwards Bishop of London. Of Lowth's *Grammar* Wesley had a good opinion, though in a letter to his brother Charles (February 1767) he said: 'Bishop Lowth is sometimes hypercritical and *finds* fault where there *is* none. Yet doubtless his is the best English Grammar that is extant.' Writing in 1764 to his friend Margaret Lewen, whom he describes in the *Journal* as 'a remarkable

[1] i.e. 'making certain', 'standardizing'.

monument of divine mercy', he gave her this advice: 'The first thing you should understand a little of is grammar; in order to which it will suffice to read first the Kingswood *English Grammar* (which is exceeding short), and then Bishop Lowth's *Introduction.*' Seventeen years later (1781) he repeats this advice, almost word for word, in a letter to Sarah Wesley, his niece, Charles's daughter. Of Priestley his opinion is not so high. In the *Journal* (17th June 1770) he writes: 'In the afternoon I looked over Dr Priestley's *English Grammar*. I wonder he could publish after Bishop Lowth's.' The remark is a little cryptic, in view of the fact that Priestley's book preceded Lowth's by a month or two; but its meaning is plain.

Certainly as a formal grammarian Wesley could not compare with Priestley or Lowth, whose substantial books are notable contributions to that developing study of the language which was characteristic of the eighteenth century. *A Short English Grammar* is Wesley's title; and it is an apt one, for the book, as he himself says, is 'exceeding short', running to only twelve pages. Contemporary grammarians—including, for example, Johnson in the short grammar prefixed to the *Dictionary*—usually divided their subject into four main parts, orthography, etymology (that is, accidence), syntax, and prosody. Wesley's treatment is too brief for such august and learned divisions as this. He concentrates on what he considered the fundamentals—accidence, with the merest hint of spelling, and a faint suggestion of syntax. His work has eight brief chapters, or sections, as he himself called them. Their titles are interesting and significant: I, Of Letters; II, Of Nouns; III, Of Pronouns; IV, Of Verbs; V, Of Auxiliary Verbs; VI, Of Regular Verbs; VII, Of Irregular Verbs; VIII, Of Adverbs, Prepositions, and Conjunctions. All these he polishes off in his few pages of brief definitions and plain dogmatic rules. Any serious treatment of syntax, idiom, and what we now call usage was outside his scope and purpose; as indeed it was outside the scope and purpose of his contemporaries and immediate predecessors. In Johnson's *Grammar* already referred to, for example, the section on syntax runs to no more than twenty lines. True, both Priestley and Lowth had recognized the importance of syntax and idiom in a language that retained only a few vestiges of inflection; and paid considerable attention to what Cobbett called 'those principles and rules which teach us how to put words together as to form *sentences*'. But Wesley was writing for children; and he was careful to give them, in as brief a space as possible, facts and forms which could be learnt by rote, like arithmetical tables, or indeed like a Latin declension. No doubt for the same reason, an exaggerated attention to inflectional rules is apparent in many school text-books even today.

Words are made up of letters; so Wesley goes back to the beginning. His first section consists of five axiomatic statements, all sound enough as far as they go. A vowel, he says, is 'a Letter that may be pronounced alone, as a, e, i, o, u'; a consonant is 'a letter that cannot be pronounced without a Vowel, as b, c, d'. What the young scholars of Kingswood made of this bald pronouncement it is difficult to imagine, since they would think instinctively of the *names* of the letters, and it would be as easy to say *b* as *a*. But this very real difficulty of the relationship between symbol and sound did not occur to Wesley, or at any rate he gave no attention to it. It had, in fact, troubled the early grammarians of the seventeenth century. Charles Butler in his *English Grammar* (1634) marvelled that *h* was named 'ache', and six years later Samuel Daines, himself a schoolmaster, discussing the alphabet, remarks naïvely and with some bewilderment, that 'F, L, M, N, R,[2] S, X, Z[3] begin their sound with E, and end in themselves'. However, Wesley goes some way towards elucidating the matter in his definition of *syllable*:

[2] Evidently, according to Daines, called 'er', since he complains that 'many Infantuli produce R *quasi* Ar'.

[3] The old name for z was 'ezard' or 'edsard'.

'a Vowel or Diphthong,[4] either single, or pronounced with a Consonant'; but even so, the children must have been a trifle puzzled. His concern is not primarily with pronunciation or what we should call phonetics, but with the actual symbols; and he rounds off this brief section, appropriately enough, with a list of the letters of the alphabet, of which, he says, there are twenty-four. The apparent discrepancy is easily explained by the fact that in the eighteenth century *i* and *j*, *u* and *v* were counted as one symbol having separate forms for vowel and consonant sounds.

In the next section Wesley proceeds to the treatment of grammar itself. Although it is entitled simply 'Of Nouns', it consists of an outline of what he himself called 'the sorts of words'. They are, he says, seven in number: 'a Noun, a Pronoun, a Verb, a Participle, an Adverb, a Conjunction, and a Preposition'. Why he includes the participle it is difficult to understand, since later in the *Grammar* he treats it, as we do, as a part of the verb. It is strange, too, at first sight that the adjective is not included in the list. But here Wesley reverts to an older tradition, when grammarians spoke of the 'noun substantive' and the 'noun adjective'. Ben Jonson, for example, in his *Grammar* (1640)[5] says, somewhat cryptically, 'All nounes are words of number, singular, or plurall. They are common, proper, personall. They are all substantive or adjective'; he also includes the participle among the parts of speech, with the introductory remark that 'in our English speech we number the same parts with the Latines'. Doctor Johnson steers a middle course, referring to 'Nouns Substantives' and 'Adjectives' as separate entities; and

[4] Like his contemporaries (Johnson, for example) Wesley means by diphthong a compound of two or more symbols (*au, owe*) representing a single sound, not a combination in one syllable of two or more sounds that may, in fact, be represented by a single symbol, like the *o* in *lone* and the *i* in *wine*. The term is still used loosely in this way, and also for the linked letters (æ, œ), now technically termed ligatures. A compound of two letters is now more properly called a digraph, and a compound of three letters a trigraph.

[5] Published posthumously.

B

Cobbett, some seventy years later, drops the term 'substantive', and speaks simply, in the modern way, of the Noun and the Adjective, without any suggestion of a grammatical relationship.

Wesley, indeed, treats of the Adjective in this section 'Of Nouns', but he admits a distinction which Ben Jonson in the passage quoted above appears to ignore. 'The Number of Nouns', he says, 'are two'; but 'all Adjectives are Indeclinable, having no variation either of Gender, Case, or Number'. He also recognizes the three degrees of comparison, the comparative degree being 'form'd by adding er to the Positive; the Superlative by adding est'. Only four adjectives, he says, break this rule—*good, bad, little, much* or *many*. He says nothing of the qualification of polysyllabic adjectives by *more* and *most*, where the inflections *-er* and *-est* produce awkward and not easily pronounceable words, though this device was, of course, established long before the eighteenth century. 'The most beautiful Lake I ever saw', he says in the *Journal*—not the *beautifullest*. But such an important refinement upon his rule the young scholars had to stumble upon for themselves. He is content to give a plain statement which, on the face of it, admits of no modification.

To return, however, to nouns proper. With his eye upon Latin, he says that there are three genders, 'the Masculine, the Feminine, and the Neuter', following this with the apparently contradictory statement 'But Nouns have no Genders'. Here, in fact, but rather (it may be surmised) by luck than by judgement, he is perfectly right. In an uninflected language like English, where there is no division of nouns into declensions according to inflectional particles, and where moreover the adjective is not inflected as it is in French, gender —as far as nouns are concerned—does not exist: such pairs as *man—woman, tiger—tigress, fox—vixen*, represent a distinction not of grammar but of vocabulary. No question of agreement is involved, except the relationship reflected in pronouns. Whether Wesley properly realized this is doubtful. At any rate, in his curt dismissal of gender he is ahead of his time. School text-books, almost up to the present day, have tended to regard gender as an integral part of English nouns.

On case he is equally brief, dogmatic, and contradictory. 'A *Case*', he says, loosely and inadequately, 'is the Variation of the last Syllable. But *Nouns* in *English* have no *Cases*.' Again he is substantially right if he means that the inflected endings of Old English have for the most part disappeared. But like other eighteenth-century grammarians Wesley reveals no knowledge of historical grammar. He does not realize that our modern apostrophe *s* represents an Old English *-es* inflection for the possessive of certain nouns; and that therefore a modern noun ending in '*s* (or *s*' in the plural)[6] may properly be said to have case in both form and function. In declaring that English nouns have no cases he rightly rejects the analogy of Latin; but in ignoring the one interesting survival of case he goes too far, and at the same time fails to give his pupils a simple rule for the apostrophe *s*, which (it must be confessed) succeeding generations of children, and, indeed, of men and women, have found singularly difficult to learn. Wesley, by the way, probably thought of the apostrophe *s* ending as a contraction of the possessive pronoun *his* following a confusion common in earlier English, represented in Shakespeare by such a phrase as 'the count his galleys' (*Twelfth Night*, III.iii.26), and surviving into the eighteenth century, especially with proper nouns, in an inscription like 'John Smith his book'.

Though he sometimes gives a succinct basic rule, Wesley rarely systematizes his so-called exceptions; he prefers (as has already been hinted) to treat them in isolation, as separate statements of fact to be learnt by heart. Thus he says, rightly, that 'the *Plural* Number of

[6] An analogical form: the Old English case-ending for the plural is not represented in Modern English.

Nouns is form'd, by adding *s* to the Singular'; but instead of showing that with certain nouns there are adjustments of spelling before the *s* is added, he implies that such adjustments have no connexion with the basic rule. '*Nouns* ending in y', he says, 'form the Plural in ies. Only those ending in a Diphthong are regular: as a Boy, Boys.' True enough, if we accept his definition of diphthong; but logically 'those ending in a Diphthong', being 'regular' required no further notice; and those ending in consonant plus *y* might have been more clearly related to the rule by some such statement as 'change *y* to *i* and add *es*'. But though he postulates on the part of his pupils a considerable knowledge of technical terms, he does not credit them with any power of simple deduction or correlation. In this, however, many later grammarians writing for schools have followed his example.

His ignorance of Old English accidence reveals itself again in his treatment of those nouns which kick over the traces, as it were, and refuse to add *s* for the plural. Actually, they are waifs and strays, mere survivals from certain Old English declensions, in one of which, for example, the characteristic plural ending was -*an*, and in another the plural was made by the 'mutation' or change of the main vowel. But this Wesley either did not know or ignored. All he can say is: 'A Man has in the plural, Men; a Woman, Women; a Child, Children; an Ox, Oxen; a Goose, Geese; a Foot, Feet; a Tooth, Teeth; a Mouse, Mice; a Louse, Lice; a Die, Dice; a Penny, Pence.' Even then, the old neuters like *sheep* and *deer*, which were originally uninflected for number, are left out. Still there is the list, such as it is—all ready, we may imagine, for the incantation of little voices. It did not occur to Wesley—indeed, it has not occurred to some school grammarians even now—that these wayward forms come to a child as part of the vocabulary he learns naturally in his ordinary speech. He does not require them thus baldly set down in a book. It is their origin which is interesting; and unless this is given, as a simple piece of historical grammar, they are better left out altogether.

In his treatment of pronouns Wesley is, for a Methodist, strangely unmethodical. To begin with, he lumps them all together, with no attempt at classification. 'There are 13', he says, 'I, thou, he; my or mine; thy or thine; his, her; our, your, their; this, that; which, who.' Even if each of the two alternatives is counted as one pronoun, his arithmetic seems to be wrong: there are, in fact, fourteen. The 'personal' pronouns (*I, thou, he*) he declines, though without any indication of function (that is, case), or any reference to the possessive forms. It is interesting to note that he gives *ye* as (apparently) the subject form of the second person plural, though that had long been displaced by *you*, the modern version of the old object form *eow*. No doubt the survival of *ye* in the Authorized Version influenced him here. As to the possessives he seems strangely at sea. He includes them in the general list mainly in their adjectival form (*her, our, your*, etc.), and says that they are 'indeclinable'; but he adds as a casual afterthought that 'Her, our, your, their, at the end of a Sentence take s, as, It is Hers.' Even more casual is his treatment of the relative pronoun. Two of its forms (*which, who*) are given among his 'thirteen'; and later on *whom* appears—'who, whom, is either *Singular* or *Plural*'. There is no mention anywhere of *whose*. 'That is often used', he says, 'for Who or Which: as, "The Man that spoke", for Who spoke.' In all this there is probably a reflection of a peculiar hesitation about the use of relative pronoun forms that goes back to Dryden, who in the revised version (1684) of his *Essay on Dramatick Poesy* had systematically substituted *who* for the *that* of the 1668 edition. Early in the eighteenth century Steele had devoted a whole *Spectator* paper to the subject:'*The Humble Petition of Who and Which.*' It was not until later after Wesley's time that form and function became in some measure standardized; and even today there are some uneasy doubts about the use of *that* and *whose*. One other sentence from the section 'Of Pronouns' must be quoted: 'We say, "Thou, Thee", when we speak to God; "You", when we speak to Men.' There is a glimpse here (unusual in this little book) of the other and, to us, more familiar Wesley.

The next four sections have to do, in one way or another, with verbs. It would be tedious to treat of them in any detail, but a few points are of special interest. Wesley's initial classification is odd. 'A *Verb*', he says, 'is a sort of Word, that expresses either Doing, and then it is called an *Active*, Suffering, and then it is called a *Passive*, or Being, and then it is called a *Neuter Verb*.' He has no conception of *transitive* and *intransitive;* and does not realize that the passive form, which he correctly describes in a later section, is a syntactical device by which the object of a transitive verb can be made subject without any change of meaning. The names of the English tenses, in spite of the *Report on Grammatical Terminology*, have never been properly standardized. Even today grammarians differ among themselves. But it is difficult to imagine what a class at Kingswood made of this: 'There are Five *Tenses*: 1. The *Present Tense*, which speaks of the Present Time; 2. The *Preterimperfect*, which speaks of the Time not perfectly past. 3. The *Preterperfect*, which speaks of the Time perfectly past. 4. The *Preterpluperfect*, which speaks of the Time which is more than perfectly past; and 5. The *Future*, which speaks of the Time to come.' Preterimperfect must have exercised their infant tongues, and the conception of a 'Time which is more than perfectly past' puzzled their simple and finite minds. However, at the end of this section (iv) he gives them a little comfort. 'There is', he adds in a kind of afterthought, 'but One *Conjugation* in *English*.' Bewildered by the conjugations in his *Latin Grammar*, they must have come upon this bald (and, indeed, unconvincing) statement with extraordinary relief.

To prove his point, in a later section (vi) ominously entitled 'Of *Regular* Verbs', he conjugates for them in full

JOHN WESLEY'S *GRAMMAR*

the verb *fear*. Once granted his odd terminology, and the fact that (in common with his contemporaries) he has no real notion of the extraordinary complications of the English tense system, this conjugation is reasonably straightforward, though for some unintelligible reason he gives the Future tense as 'I shou'd have feared'. But before this (Section V—'Of Auxiliary Verbs') he must have dashed their hopes with long and complicated conjugations of *have* and *be*, together with those of the 'Defective ones', *can, may, shall, will, must, ought*, and what he rather cryptically calls the 'old Auxiliary Verb' *do*. One or two minor points are of interest. He consistently uses the spellings *cou'd* and *wou'd*, an interesting phonetic variant common in the eighteenth century and earlier. In the future tense he gives *shall* and *will* as alternatives for all persons, as does Cobbett sixty years afterwards. The nice distinction between the two, to which Fowler devotes three or four learned columns, had not yet arisen. For the subject of the verb in the second person plural he uses the form *ye*, as he does in the declension of pronouns (see p. 17). There are, rather surprisingly, a couple of misprints in this section. Two sub-divisions are numbered '9', and for the second person singular of the Preterpluperfect of *have* he gives the odd form 'Thou had hadst'.

The subjunctive forms of the verb always tended to give eighteenth-century grammarians a little trouble, mainly because they had no knowledge of the original Old English inflections. Only a few Old English forms survived in the eighteenth century (and still survive)—the third person singular, without inflection ('if he speak' as distinct from the indicative 'he speaks') and the forms *be* and *were* throughout the singular of the Present and the Past (Wesley's Imperfect) tenses respectively of the verb *be*, which, of course, may occur in all compound tenses containing *be* as an auxiliary. Cobbett, speaking particularly of the verb *be*, says simply that 'the subjunctive, in all its persons, takes the infinitive of the verb without any change at all', and seems to regard 'if he be' as a contraction of 'if he may be'. Wesley does not even recognize the surviving forms. His subjunctives are always compounds with *may* and *might*—'if he may be', 'if he might have'. This is a little surprising, especially as the old simple subjunctive inflections (which paradoxically had no characteristic ending) were far more common in the writing of the eighteenth century than they are today; and even modern grammarians have at least to mention them, if only because of the surviving use of *were* after *if*, in such expressions as 'if this were to happen' and 'if I were you'.

On participles Wesley is incomprehensible. 'A *Participle*', he says, 'is a Sort of Word that has *Numbers, Genders*, and *Cases* like a Noun, and *Tenses* like a *Verb.*' That a participle should have tenses may be granted. We still speak, though somewhat illogically, of a present participle ('going') and a past participle ('gone'). But how a word like *seeing* or *broken* can have '*Numbers, Genders*, and *Cases* like a Noun' Wesley does not trouble to explain. It is all the more puzzling because he has already declared that nouns themselves have neither genders nor cases.

Most of the so-called 'irregular' verbs in modern English are survivals of those verbs, usually called 'strong' by grammarians today, in which the past forms (tense and participle), are made by a change of the main vowel—*shake —shook—shaken, drink—drank—drunk, break—broke—broken*, and the like. Their other characteristic was that the past participle ended in *-en* (not -[e]d as in 'regular' verbs), which is sometimes lost in modern English, as in *rung* for *rungen*. None of the older grammarians understood this, and so could do no more than set down these verbal rebels in alphabetical lists, in the hope, presumably, that the bewildered reader would learn them by heart. Wesley's list is in Section VII, '*Of Irregular* Verbs'. Since he does not give a line apiece to the individual verbs, it is a most forbidding mass of words. He includes in it not only the strong verbs, but also those 'weak' (*-ed*) verbs which have irregular forms owing to contractions, such as *sent* for *sended*, *leapt* for *leaped*, and *felt* for *feeled*, or vowel changes which arose for a different phonological reason, such as *sought* and *sold*. But his true 'strong' forms have a special interest, and deserve a paragraph or two to themselves.

In the mid-eighteenth century there was a marked tendency to bring the past participle of strong verbs into line with the past tense, where it had, in normal use, differed from it. Thus, to give a notable example, Gray's original title for his best-known poem was 'Elegy, wrote in a Country Churchyard', the tense form *wrote* standing for the participle form *written*. In the *Grammar* Wesley gives *written* for the past participle; yet he himself often used *wrote*:—'To one who had many times wrote to me on this head' (20th May 1739), 'Need any one ask from what motive this was wrote?' (11th November 1775). For the tense he uses *writ* and *wrote* indifferently: 'I writ the trustees for Georgia an account of our year's expense' (4th March 1737); 'The letter I wrote was as follows' (5th March 1767). In respect of this verb and others his precept and practice reflect a certain fluidity of usage existing before the standardization that was soon to assert itself and remains today.

There are a few other interesting forms in Wesley's list, notably *bad* (from *bid*), *bit*, *ran*, *rose*, *shook*, *strove*, and *took*, for the participle, and *rung*, *shrunk*, *stunk*, for the tense. He does not include the verb *sink*, but in the *Journal* he consistently uses the tense form *sunk*, as, for example, 'She sunk down as before (23rd October 1739) and 'The floor sunk no further' (1st October 1741). One or two other usages in the *Journal* are of interest:

'Our clothes were soon froze together' (23rd December 1736).
'which indeed I had forgot' (3rd November 1737).
'Some have believed, and began to run well' (3rd February 1738).

'having rode over a narrow foot-bridge' (14th March 1738).

'We were overtook by an elderly gentleman' (21st March 1738).

'After I had spoke about a quarter of an hour' (25th May 1750).

'Surely this time will not soon be forgotten' (16th June 1764).

'a window near the pulpit being taken down' (22nd July 1764).

It is possible that the variants *forgot—forgotten*, and (*over*)*took—taken* represent a change of usage in the quarter of a century that separates them. But the simpler explanation is that the form used was, to adapt a famous remark of Sam Weller, according to the taste and fancy of the writer. In the *Grammar*, for example, Wesley gives *frozen, spoken* without alternative, as the past participles of *freeze, speak*, though he himself uses *froze, spoke* in the quotations given above. He also gives *begun* as the past participle form of *begin*; but in the sentence quoted he uses *began*, unless this is, in fact, by some rather strained syntax, a past tense. (See also p. 39.)

The list also contains a few oddities. The past participle of *bleed* is given as *blooded*, of *die* as *dead*, and (to the comfort of many since who have fallen into the same error) of *lie* as *laid*. As the tense and participle form of *work*, he gives *wrought*, again, no doubt, with memories of the Authorized Version, since the 'regular' form had already established itself in the literal sense. He uses the spelling *chuse*, familiar in Jane Austen, for the modern *choose* which is the form, in *Johnson's Dictionary* (see p. 40); and by what is (we trust) a misprint he gives *loose* as the present corresponding with the past (tense and participle) form *lost*.

The Wesley hymns reflect here and there these old and pleasant confusions, sometimes for the sake of rhythm and rhyme. We still sing (M.H.B. 721):

> *A band of love, a threefold cord,*
> *Which never can be broke,*

although the *Grammar* says that *broken* is the past participle. 'Wrestling Jacob' (M.H.B. 339) has the lines:

> *In vain I have not wept and strove;*
> *Thy nature and thy name is love,*

and, in the original (1780) edition of the *Hymns,*

> *The Sun of Righteousness on me*
> *Hath rose with healing in his wings,*

where the modern editors (M.H.B. 339) have substituted *risen* for *rose*. The variants *showed—shown* were particularly convenient for rhyme. *Showed* was frequently used, somewhat loosely, as a rhyme for *God*, thus (M.H.B. 343):

> *Whoe'er to Thee themselves approve*
> *Must take the path Thy word hath showed,*
> *Justice pursue, and mercy love,*
> *And humbly walk by faith with God.*

But *shown* was available when rhyme demanded (*Hymns,* 1780, No. ciii):

> *Let me be by grace restored,*
> *On me be all long-suffering shown:*
> *Turn, and look upon me, Lord,*
> *And break my heart of stone.*

There was, also in the *Hymns* (1780), yet another refinement: the alternative spellings *shew, shew'd* were used to rhyme with such words as *do, good* (No. cxxxi):

> *If still thou goest about to do*
> *Thy needy creatures good,*
> *On me, that thy praise may shew,*
> *Be all thy wonders shew'd*[7]

---

[7] *show, showed* in M.H.B. (1904). The hymn is not in the present *Methodist Hymn-book*.

To sum up, all such abnormalities (judged, that is, by present usage) whether in Wesley's prose or in the *Hymns*, were merely indicative of a particular transitional stage in the history of the language. The Kingswood children, slowly and carefully getting by heart their irregular verbs, might have been comforted by the fact—had they but known it—that Wesley sometimes ignored the rules of his own *Grammar*.

At the end of this Section (VII) Wesley states one of his rare syntactical rules: 'A Verb must always be of the same *Number* and *Person*, with the *Noun* or *Pronoun* going before it: As, "I love You. Christians love one another".' The second example, we may imagine, is a kind of indirect precept, directed at the members of Kingswood, both boys and masters. But it is curious that, in fact, the two sentences illustrate nothing at all. Wesley did not realize that, to make his meaning plain, he must use different inflectional forms, with their appropriate subjects, of the verb *to love*.

The last Section (VIII) is called 'Of Adverbs, Prepositions, and Conjunctions'. It is only about a dozen lines long; thus cavalierly does Wesley treat these particles which play so important a part in syntax and idiom. An adverb 'is added to a *Verb*, to perfect, explain or inlarge its Sense'; he mentions no other adverbial function. 'Adverbs', he says, 'are compared like *Noun Adjectives*,' which is manifestly untrue of most adverbs, including all those which have the characteristic ending *-ly*. He reckons among adverbs 'those Words which are commonly called *Interjections*: as, ah! oh!'. A preposition he defines vaguely (perhaps remembering Dryden) as 'a Sort of Word which is commonly set before another, or compounded with it, as, go *to* London'. And the book ends with the bland statement that 'A Conjunction is a Sort of Word, which joins Words or Sentences together: as *and*, *or*.'

So much, then, for the *Grammar*. In one sense it is characteristic of Wesley. It is, we feel, purposely, almost

JOHN WESLEY'S *GRAMMAR* 25

religiously, dryasdust. Kingswood was a place for work; games, indeed, were expressly forbidden. The bare, unadorned, usually unexplained statements of this little book were exactly those which would discipline the memory and the tender minds of those young pupils during their interminable days of lessons, manual labour, and prayers. To him grammar without tears would have savoured a little of the wicked one. But in another respect it is uncharacteristic. As has been shown in the previous pages, the *Grammar* bristles with inconsistencies, inaccuracies, and obvious errors. There is little trace of logical principles in either its contents or its arrangement. We can only surmise that Wesley had very little understanding of the mechanics of a language which he himself uses not so much with elegance as with clear and forthright effect.

II

John Wesley's *Dictionary*

THERE is something disarming, as well as amusing, about the words on the title-page of the *Dictionary*: 'The author assures you he thinks this is the best English dictionary in the world.' We cannot but admire an author who is so confident of his qualifications and so certain of his wares. But it has to be read, if we are to understand its significance, in conjunction with the Preface. There, in his own forthright way, Wesley announces his intentions, deals faithfully with his contemporary rivals, and explains the uncompromising N.B. to the reader. In order that, at the outset, we may appreciate the background, as it were, of a work so magnificently recommended by the lexicographer himself, the Preface to the first edition and the Postscript which he added in the second are printed in full:

TO THE READER

As incredible as it may appear, I must avow, that this dictionary is not published to get money, but to assist persons of common sense and no learning, to understand the best *English* authors: and that, with as little expence of either time or money, as the nature of the thing would allow.
To this end it contains, not a heap of *Greek* and *Latin* words, just tagged with *English* terminations: (for no good *English* writer, none but vain or senseless pedants, give these any place in their writings): not a scroll of barbarous *law expressions*, which are neither *Greek*, *Latin*, nor good *English*: not a croud of *technical* terms, the meaning whereof is to be sought in books expressly wrote on the subjects to which they belong: not such English words as *and*, *of*, *but*; which stand so gravely in Mr *Bailey's*, *Pardon's*, and *Martin's* dictionaries: but 'most of those hard words which are found in the best *English*

writers.' I say, *most*; for I purposely omit not only all which are not *hard*, and which are not found in the best writers: not only all law-words and most technical terms, but likewise all, the meaning of which may be easily gathered from those of the same derivation. And this I have done, in order to make this dictionary both as short and as cheap as possible.

I should add no more, but that I have so often observed, the only way, according to the modern taste, for any author to procure commendation to his book is, vehemently to commend it himself. For want of this deference to the publick, several excellent tracts lately printed, but left to commend themselves by their intrinsic worth, are utterly unknown or forgotten. Whereas if a writer of tolerable sense will but bestow a few violent encomiums on his own work, especially if they are skilfully ranged in the title-page, it will pass thro' six editions in a trice; the world being too complaisant to give a gentleman the Lie, and taking it for granted, he understands his own performance best.

In compliance therefore with the taste of the age, I add, that this little dictionary is not only the shortest and the cheapest, but likewise, by many degrees, the most correct which is extant at this day. Many are the mistakes in all the other *English* dictionaries which I have yet seen. Whereas I can truly say, I know of none in this; and I conceive the reader will believe me: for if I had, I should not have left it there. Use then this help, till you find a better.
Oct. 1753.

In this Edition I have added some hundreds of words, which were omitted in the former: chiefly from Mr *Johnson's* dictionary, which I carefully looked over for that purpose. And I will now venture to affirm, that, small as it is, this dictionary is quite sufficient, for enabling any one to understand the best writings now extant, in the English tongue.
Oct. 20, 1763.

Now it may be deduced from this that, being a lover not only of good English but also of common sense, he keeps clearly in mind the people who will be likely to use his dictionary. They are those who, with little schooling, have by dint of concentration and hard toil learnt to read, 'persons of common sense and no learning'. It is not fanciful to imagine that in his thought there are the men and women of those new Methodist societies which by his own labours, under God, were even then being established up and down the land. For them, in such time as he could snatch from his crowded days of journeying and preaching, he had himself prepared and edited a considerable amount of devotional literature; since, recognizing the importance of both the written and the spoken word, he was author and publisher as well as preacher. And what, after all, would these simple folk require? They were acquainted with all the common, ordinary words; and they had no use for the derivatives—'Greek and Latin words just tagged with English terminations'—or technical terms which were beginning to jostle one another in the learned and scientific writing of the eighteenth century. So, very wisely, Wesley set his bounds. The common words he excluded because they were already known; the learned words because, by the people he was providing for, they need never be known at all. And by keeping his *Dictionary* short, he was able to make it cheap. To Wesley that was a matter of the highest importance. The people whom he wished to help were, he knew, in the main poor people. It was no use preparing a book they could not buy. He stresses the same point in the Preface to the *Hymns* (1780). During the years the collection had grown, since more variety was needed for those 'among whom singing makes so considerable a part of the public service'; but the volume of 1780 'is not so large', he declares, 'as to be either cumbersome or expensive'. Wesley's *Dictionary* (like the *Hymns*) was intended for, and no doubt found its way into, lowly cottages and humble homes. We cannot properly judge it or appreciate its true value unless we remember that.

Certainly, like the *Grammar* the *Dictionary* is 'exceeding short'. The second edition (1764), even with 'some hundreds of words' added, 'chiefly from Mr *Johnson's* dictionary', runs to no more than 150 pages. There are fewer than six thousand entries, and only occasionally

JOHN WESLEY'S *DICTIONARY* 29

does an entry take up more than one line. Wesley gives no guide to pronunciation except marks of stress, no indication of parts of speech, and no etymologies. The word is followed by the definition, and the definition alone. Here, as in many other ways, he is severely practical. The people who used his dictionary would, he rightly assumed, be interested only in meaning; they were not concerned with function, grammar, or etymology.

Wesley's self-advertisement on the title-page, and his ironically humorous (almost Swiftian) comment on it in the Preface are a trifle unusual even for those days. But his scarcely veiled contempt for his predecessors only reflects the open, almost cut-throat, rivalry of the eighteenth-century lexicographers. The three to whom Wesley specifically refers, Nathaniel Bailey, Benjamin Martin, and William Pardon, in long and elaborate titles proclaimed either directly or by implication their superiority to others. And indeed not entirely without reason; for each in turn spread his net wider, recognized the swiftly growing vocabulary that reflected the broadening interests and increasing complications of contemporary life, and added new guides to pronunciation, function, and (sometimes) etymology. Bailey, for example, boasts that his *Universal Etymological English Dictionary* comprehends 'the Derivations of the Generality of Words in the English Tongue, either Antient or Modern, from the Antient British, Saxon, Danish, Norman and Modern French, Teutonic, Dutch, Spanish, Italian, Latin, Greek and Hebrew Languages, each in their proper characters, and also a Brief and clear Explication of all difficult Words derived from any of the aforesaid Languages; and Terms of Art relating to Anatomy, Botany, Physick, Pharmacy, Surgery, Chymistry, Philosophy, Divinity, Mathematicks, Grammar, Logick, Rhetorick, Musick, Heraldry, Maritime Affairs, Military Discipline, Horsemanship, Hunting, Hauking, Fowling, Fishing, Gardening, Husbandry, Handicrafts, Confectionery, Carving, Cookery, etc.'. Both

Martin and Pardon make equally comprehensive claims, adding certain refinements and characteristics peculiar to themselves. They were, indeed, the pioneers of scientific lexicography, imperfect, unscholarly often, sometimes wrong—but pointing the way. In the year in which Wesley's *Dictionary* was published (1753) Doctor Johnson was bringing to an end that *English Dictionary* which was the culmination of them all, written (as he said) 'with little assistance of the learned, and without any patronage of the great; not in the soft obscurities of retirement, or under the shelter of academick bowers, but amid inconvenience and distraction, in sickness and sorrow'. It is interesting to imagine what Wesley thought when, two hundred years ago, this masterpiece—still in a real sense the greatest of all English dictionaries—was given to the world.

We have to remember that Wesley's *Dictionary* is in no way to be compared with the larger, more comprehensive dictionaries of his time, though in his somewhat ungenerous references to Bailey and the rest he himself hardly seems to recognize the fact. His own argument for the limitation of words and simplicity of treatment in a dictionary intended for ordinary unlearned people is not, however, without cogency: most modern 'concise' dictionaries are, indeed, far too elaborate in their dealings with common words. But Wesley laid about him with typical Wesley courage. Out went everything which he considered irrelevant and unnecessary. His dictionary was not intended to be a full and academic record of the language, but a handbook to help people to read and write. If this is granted, it had some claim to be, as Mr Eric Partridge has reminded us,[1] 'the best small dictionary in English' of its time.

Still, though we recognize the *Dictionary* as adequate for his purpose, to us it is a little disappointing in another way. As in the *Grammar*, Wesley is matter-of-fact and utilitarian; 'he aims not at wit', says Partridge, 'nor at

[1] *London Quarterly and Holborn Review*, October 1932; *Proceedings of the Wesley Historical Society*, December 1950.

JOHN WESLEY'S *DICTIONARY* 31

originality'. Yet, after all, the very brevity and directness of his definitions are characteristic of the man. It is interesting to take a few words which in retrospect have a peculiar significance, and compare his own laconic entries with those of his contemporaries or immediate predecessors.[2] For *Methodist* he has, briefly and simply, 'one that lives according to the method laid down in the bible'. Bailey (1721) was too early for the specialized meaning, but Martin (1749) has as a second definition 'a fanatick, or one that pretends to be inspired'. Johnson (1755) thus defines the word in unmistakable accents: '3. One of a new kind of Puritans lately arisen, so called from their profession to live by rules and in constant method', and Pardon (1771), always verbose and encyclopaedic, goes into some detail: 'one that acts or does things by a particular mode, manner, or rule; there are now a set of persons who call themselves Methodists, and pretend to more sanctity and purity of life than other people, and go about preaching, singing psalms, hymns, etc., in the fields, streets, and private houses'. There is something peculiarly moving in Wesley's definition, unpretentious as it is, in the light of the others.

Under the word *enthusiasm* the *Shorter Oxford English Dictionary* has the note: 'In 18th c. often: Ill-regulated religious emotion or speculation.' The term was, of course, often associated with the Methodists, who were sneeringly dubbed *enthusiasts*. Johnson has: '*enthusiast*: One who vainly imagines a private revelation; one who has a vain confidence of his intercourse with God', and the other definitions are in the same key, including Wesley's own: 'a religious madman, one that fancies himself inspired'.[3] Partridge, quoting this with the comment,

[2] Mr Partridge gives some of these examples, with brief comments, in his article referred to above, to which I am much indebted.

[3] There is an interesting antithesis in Hymn 94 (1780):

> *The same in your esteem*
> *Falsehood and truth ye join,*
> *The wild enthusiast's idle dream,*
> *And real work divine.*

'Wesley knew that he was often described thus', seems to imply that Wesley is writing in defiant and sorrowful irony. And that indeed may be so. It was at Epworth itself that he heard the curate, Mr Romley, say that 'one of the most dangerous ways of quenching the Spirit was by enthusiasm', and 'enlarge on the character of an enthusiast in a very florid and oratorical manner'; whereupon, as if to refute the implied charge, he proceeded boldly to preach (being denied the church) on his father's tombstone.[4] Once, at Seven Dials, having had a service of five hours 'added to his usual employment', he wondered whether his strength would stand the strain. 'But God', he says, 'looked to that: so I must think; and they that will call it enthusiasm may.' Thus as a lexicographer he accepts the current meaning of the term, but as a preacher boldly endows it with a new significance. It is tempting to think that Johnson, had he been a follower of Wesley, would have allowed (as he often did) a personal and individual definition here. Faithful to the etymology, he would have written, we may imagine, something on these lines: '*enthusiast*, a person filled with the Spirit of God; a Methodist'.

On *justification* Wesley is brief—'forgiveness of sins; vindication'—as is Johnson with '3. Deliverance by pardon from sins past'. Bailey (and Martin, who copies Bailey's definition almost exactly), is a little more elaborate: '*Justification* (in *Divinity*) is a Clearing of Transgressors of the Divine Laws, by the Imputation of Christ's Righteousness'; and Pardon, in his usual verbose manner, paraphrases and elaborates their definition. Wesley on *conversion* is explicit: 'a thorough change of heart and life from sin to holiness, a turning', but has not the forthright antithesis of Johnson: 'a change from reprobation to grace, from a bad to a holy life'. It seems, indeed, a little cold and academic against the background of the 'heart strangely warmed'. But the *Dictionary* was not the *Journal*. Again, it is characteristic of Wesley that he kept them apart.

Many of the other definitions are interesting, reflecting

[4] *Journal*, 5th June 1742.

the man and his period. An Arminian is 'one that believes universal redemption'; Calvinists (for some odd reason in the plural) 'they that hold absolute, unconditional Predestination'. Wesley's own Arminianism comes out in his definition of *the elect*, 'all that truly believe in Christ'. Here Bailey is ambiguous: '(among *Divines*) the Faithful, the elected Saints'. Johnson has a Calvinistic definition: '(in theology) chosen as an object of eternal mercy', and Pardon is in the same strain wordily explicit: 'according to some schemes of Divinity, those persons pre-ordained to salvation, without any regard to their obeying or disobeying the commands of laws of God, from all eternity, are called the elect'.

Of a Dissenter Wesley says that 'he refuses communion of the Church of England', and of a Nonconformist that he is a 'dissenter from the church'. That has a special interest when we remember that three years after the *Dictionary* was published he made this entry in the *Journal*: 'My brother and I closed the Conference by a solemn declaration of our purpose never to separate from the Church; and all our brethren concurred therein.' A Puritan, on the other hand, is (rather surprisingly) 'an old, strict Church of England man'—a description which seems strangely at variance with our common ideas, and with Johnson's definition: 'a sectary pretending to eminent purity of religion'.[5]

It seems at first a little odd that he does not include the word *watch-night*. But the reason is not far to seek; it was a word that all his own people understood, and therefore did not qualify for inclusion. But he does give 'watch-night' as a definition of the corresponding Latin *vigil*, with the explanation: 'the primitive Christians observed such before all the great festivals'. The word does not appear in Johnson or the other eighteenth-century dictionaries. In the *Shorter Oxford English Dictionary*, the first definition is 'orig. a religious service extending over

[5] The Johnson definitions quoted are often taken from the Concise version of his *Dictionary*, which he published in 1786.

midnight held monthly by Wesleyan Methodists', which seems to imply that the word was coined by the early Methodists, probably by Wesley himself. At any rate, it was a happy and indeed beautiful invention; for it is not fanciful to associate it with the stirring question 'Watchman, what of the night?' and the cry of the watch through the city streets. The word has a peculiar evocative quality in the light of Wesley's own description:

We had the first watch-night in London. We commonly choose for this solemn service the Friday night nearest the full moon, either before or after, that those of the congregation who live at a distance may have light to their several homes. The service begins at half-an-hour past eight, and continues to a little after midnight. We have often found a peculiar blessing at these seasons. There is generally a deep awe upon the congregation, perhaps in some measure owing to the silence of the night, particularly in singing the hymn with which we commonly conclude:

> *Hearken to the solemn voice,*
> *The awful midnight cry!*
> *Wailing souls, rejoice, rejoice,*
> *And feel the bridegroom nigh.*

Three or four other interesting definitions have an ecclesiastical flavour, or are more or less closely related to the religious conditions of the time. A rural dean, he says wryly, is 'a Clergyman appointed to observe the behaviour of other Clergymen'. Deism, the fashionable creed of the eighteenth century, is bluntly described as 'infidelity denying the Bible'. Johnson is more precise though slightly ambiguous: 'The opinion of those that only acknowledge one God, without the reception of any revealed religion.' Behind his definition of *missionary*, which is strictly etymological, there is perhaps a hint of autobiography: 'one sent to preach the gospel.' A chaplet he dismisses briefly as 'popish beads'; and a directory is 'a book of directions for prayer' with no reference (as in Johnson) to its origin in the 'factious preachers' of the rebellion. Here and there we light upon a word which has become familiar to us in the hymns. *Beatifick*, he says, is 'making happy: but it is only used in reference to heaven'. For *antepast*, that strange and misleading word which rings finely in the joy of the conversion hymn:

> *Should know, should taste my sins forgiven,*
> *Blest with the antepast of heaven!*

he gives simply 'foretaste'. The *Shorter Oxford* has its original and literal meaning, 'a whet taken before a meal',[6] and illustrates the figurative sense with a quotation from Horace Walpole. We have lost the word now; most modern concise dictionaries have no mention of it. It is interesting to note, by the way, while hymns are in our mind, that for *organ* he gives merely 'an instrument: so the eye is the organ of sight', and makes no specific reference to music. This is, however, scarcely surprising, since even in the Anglican churches of the eighteenth century this instrument 'consisting of pipes filled with wind, and of stops touched by the hand' (as Johnson has it) was not at all common; and it certainly had no place in the Foundery, the New Room, or the humble meeting-places up and down the land. However, *precentor* is in the *Dictionary*—'he that begins the tune in the choir'; and we are reminded that at the Methodist Conference the organ, though it may be magnificently present to the eye, remains dumb and silent still.

Outside the religious and ecclesiastical realm there are one or two interesting definitions. For *coquet* he has 'a woman affectedly airy, seeking to make conquests', which faintly echoes Johnson's lighthearted 'a gay airy girl; a girl who endeavours to attract attention'. Though throughout the *Journal* he is severe on plays, theatres, and frivolous amusements, no hint of his displeasure reveals itself, for example, in his definition of *comedy*, 'a merry play', or *coopee*, 'a step in dancing'. Here and there we get a glimpse of eighteenth-century fashion, but briefly, without elaboration. A *bannian* is 'a sort of nightgown', a

[6] Latin *ante*, 'before' + *pascere*, 'nourish'. Cf. *repast*.

fardingale 'a whalebone circle on which ladies formerly tied their petticoats; a sort of hoop', and a *cuerpo*, 'a waistcoat'. He ignores the idiom 'be (or walk) in cuerpo', which Johnson defines pontifically 'be without the upper coat, so as to discover the shape of the *cuerpo* or body', and Bailey more simply and vividly 'go without a cloak, as if to show one's shapes'. The definition of *manufactures*, 'works made by the hand', and a *mechanic*, 'a tradesman', takes us back to a world before—though by only a few years—the onset of the Industrial Revolution; so too, but in a more remote and general way, does *curfew*, 'the eight o'clock bell'.

A few words have a now obsolescent or obsolete meaning that points backwards to their origin or forward to the modern sense. Thus *to balderdash* is 'to adulterate, mix': so Johnson, 'to mix or adulterate any liquor'. Oddly enough, neither Wesley nor Johnson has the noun; but Bailey gives it, with a definition that indicates how its meaning was already moving from the literal ('mixture of liquors'—*Concise Oxford Dictionary*) to the figurative: 'a mingle-mangle, a confused Discourse'. *Ballots* are 'little balls given in votes'; but *ballot* as noun and verb, with the associated sense 'vote', is not included. *Philology* has its old (and then current) sense 'the study of polite literature: criticism', and *grammar* is significantly, 'the art of speaking and writing properly'. For *humorist* Wesley gives only the modern sense, 'a merry, whimsical man', but Johnson's definition reflects the old conception, common in Chaucer and Shakespeare, of the physical 'humours' or fluids in the body that reveal themselves in personality and conduct. On the other hand, for *museum* he has the single definition, 'a study', a sense which, according to the *Shorter Oxford Dictionary*, was obsolete by 1760. Here and there a form survives that is represented only by a derivative today: *to cark*, 'to be anxiously careful', and *nocent*, 'hurtful, guilty', are examples. Only the negative of *nocent* survives (*innocent*); and *cark* has bequeathed us nothing but its participial adjective in 'carking care'. It is significant that for *aggravate* he gives

JOHN WESLEY'S *DICTIONARY* 37

as a second meaning 'provoke', an answer to the purists who seem to regard the use of the word in that sense ('aggravate a person', 'an aggravating fellow') as a modern solecism. Now and then he throws off a refreshingly homely definition. For *cone*, which the *Concise Oxford Dictionary* (1950) defines as 'solid figure with circular (or other curved) base, tapering to a point (generated by straight line that always passes through a fixed point, and describes any fixed curve), he has simply 'anything in the form of a sugar-loaf';[7] and for *iliac passion* (one of the many terms in the *Dictionary* that bear witness to his interest in and knowledge of medicine) he has 'the twisting of the guts'.

So much for definitions. Laconic and brief as they are, they have a peculiar interest of their own, especially when it is remembered for whom the *Dictionary* was compiled.

Beyond the definitions there is nothing to comment on, except the spelling. Wesley was compiling his *Dictionary* in the years immediately preceding the publication (1755) of Johnson's; and it contains a few interesting divergences from the spelling which Johnson, except in a few minor details, bequeathed to us. Of spelling Johnson had a significant thing to say in his Preface:

In adjusting the Orthography, which has been to this time unsettled and fortuitous, I found it necessary to distinguish those irregularities that are inherent in our tongue, and perhaps coeval with it, from others which the ignorance or negligence of later writers has produced. Every language has its anomalies, which though inconvenient, and in themselves once unnecessary, must be tolerated among the imperfections of human things, and which require only to be registered, that they may not be increased, and ascertained, that they may not be confounded: but every language has likewise its improprieties and absurdities, which it is the duty of the lexicographer to correct or proscribe.

It so happens that he retained (though not altogether consistently) a few forms that were already, in his day,

[7] 'Conical moulded mass of sugar', *Concise Oxford Dictionary*.

obsolescent. In his *Art of Reading and Writing English: or, The Chief Principles and Rules of Pronouncing our Mother Tongue; with a Variety of Instructions for True Spelling*, written over twenty years before, Isaac Watts had noted that the *k* could be dropped in words ending in *-ck*, and that *u* could remain or be dropped, at will, in words like *labour* and *favour*. It is words of these two types that represent most obviously a Johnsonian spelling which has not survived. In the *Dictionary* Wesley follows him, for the most part, in retaining the final *k*—he has, for example, *aquatick, arctick, ascetick, critick*, but *mechanic*. Like Johnson himself, he is not consistent in his use of *-o(u)r*, writing for example, *labour—labor* and *favour—favor* indiscriminately. In his retention of the ligature *æ* he is more conservative than Johnson, who keeps it in unusual words— *œcumenical*, for example, which had not then entered into the popular vocabulary. He observes that '*o* is united to *e* in some words derived from Greek, as *œconomy*; but *æ* not being an English diphthong, they are better written as they are sounded, with only *e, economy*'. Accordingly, he gives *economy* in the body of the *Dictionary*, though for some not very understandable reason he has beside it *œconomicks*. Wesley sticks to *œconomy*. He also has *æ* in *dæmon* and *phænomenon*.

Other variants mentioned by Watts, *in-* and *en-*, *im-* and *em-*, *-ise* and *-ize*, are reflected in Wesley's *Dictionary*. Thus he has, like Pardon, Bailey, and Martin, *indue, inroll, inthral, invenom*. Johnson points the modern way with *enrol*, and *envenom*, but he keeps *inthrall*. The doubt remains in modern English in the pair *inquire—enquire*, but most other words have settled down to either *-en* or *-in*.

The eighteenth-century use of *s* and *z*, especially in the verbal terminations *-ise* and *-ize*, is curious, especially in view of the modern pedantic practice by which verbs ultimately derived from Greek (with the *-izein* termination) have *z*, and a few not so derived have *s*. In Fowler's definitive list of the *-ise* verbs, *exercise, chastise, devise*, and *enterprise* are included; but all of these, says Watts, may be spelt with a *z*. So, in the eighteenth century (as, for example, in Jane Austen), could the most familiar of them all, *surprise*. As it happens, not many of these words are included in the *Dictionary;* but it is noteworthy that in the 1738 text of the Sermon 'Salvation by Faith', which has only one or two departures from modern spelling, we have *comprize*, and that though the third edition of the *Hymns* (1780) has *surprise* (No. 278) the first has *surprize*.

It will be interesting at this point to illustrate from the text of the 1780 *Collection* a few other spelling variants. The *Dictionary* has *beatifick*, but *beatific* appears, like *mystic*, *gigantic*, and one or two others, without a *k*, in the hymns —an indication of an inconsistency common in Wesley as in other mid-eighteenth-century writers, or possibly of a change in convention over the period of some twenty-five years. Even more interesting are certain differences in spelling between the first and the third editions:

Hymn	1st Edn	3rd Edn	Remarks
9 v. 10	veils	vails	Perhaps a misprint.
12 v. 2	ours	our's	The apostrophe in pronominal possessives is often retained in the eighteenth century where it is dropped today. See p. 46.
97 v. 2	displicence	displacence	A misprint in the first edition. The word means displeasure—the 'opposite' of *complacence*.
128 v. 3	controul	control	But (1st Edn.) *uncontroléd* in 267 and *control* in 278.
136 v. 1	Unknow	unknown	An odd misprint in the greatest of all Charles Wesley's poems.
209 v. 2	began	begun	A remarkable syntactical example. See p. 22. The participle form is used for rhyme's sake: When he first the work *begun* Small and feeble was his day; Now the word doth swiftly *run* . . . and is retained in the present Hymn Book.
221 v. 2	chearfully	cheerfully	

Hymn	1st Edn	3rd Edn	Remarks
226 v. 3	cloathest	clothest	Watts notices the variation *oa*— *o*+*consonant*+*e* in words with the long open o sound, and gives as examples *coal—cole, cloak—cloke, smoak—smoke; shoar—shore. Smoaking* appears in Hymn 281 in both editions. We still keep the variants *cloak—cloke*.
261 v. 2	pour-trayed	portrayed	
261 v. 3	believe	belive	No doubt a misprint. Watts, however, says that *belief* can be spelt *beleef; niece, neece;* and *thieves, theeves.*
268 v. 5	entrance	entèrance	The mark of elision above the *e* is explained on p. 45. Both editions have *hinderances* in hymns 139, 140, 146. On the title page of the 1st Edn. we have 'Printed by J. Paramore, at the Foundry', but in the 3rd, 'at the Foundery'. Our present Hymn Book keeps the *e* in 'The "Foundery" Collection'.
286 v. 2	antient	anncient	
291 v. 2	fervour	fervor	
308 v. 1	lose	loose	In the *Dictionary* John Wesley has *loose* for *lose*.

Other interesting spellings, common to both editions are: *disburthened* (94), *faultèring* (109), *incompast* (124), *gulph* (126), *rent* for *rend* ('O that wouldèst the heavens rent', rhyming with *Omnipotent*—134), *it's* for *its* (136, 138), *inrollèd* (221), *lillies* (226), *œconomy* (253), *skreen* (263— but *screen* in 283), *sooth* for *soothe* (270), *smoaking* (281), *recal* (300), *chuse* (316), and *center* (498).

But to return to the *Dictionary* itself. There are several points of interest in its spelling, and some of them are noteworthy because in his practice Wesley sometimes does not follow his own precepts. But in this he did not differ from other writers of the time. Johnson is inconsistent in the *Dictionary;* and inconsistency is, after all, symbolic of this last period in the language immediately before spelling became fixed in its modern form. Moreover, there are two things to be remembered: first, that then as now printing conventions determined to a large extent the spelling of the printed word, and, second, that the actual spelling of the writer himself was at this particular time affected by a habit of abbreviation concerning which something is said later in this chapter (p. 43).

A few spellings, apart from those already mentioned, observe an already passing convention. He keeps, for example, the *t* in *atchieve* and *batchelor*, and has *c* for *s* in *frankincence*, *w* for *u* in *overhawl*, *y* for *e* in *alchymy*, *c* for *k* in *sceleton*, and *y* for *ie* in *pybald*. Here and there what appear to be mis-spellings occur; *assasinate* and *calender* are examples. Sometimes he has a kind of perverse originality. Thus, while Bailey, Johnson, and the rest have *burrow* in the modern fashion, Wesley had *burrough;* on the other hand, though they have *furlough*, he has *furlow*. He makes an interesting distinction, not observed by Johnson, between *center*, verb, and *centre*, noun; the verb spelling has already been noted in the 1780 *Hymns*. Now and then, double letters (now single) appear, as in *conn*, *imbecillity*, and *ribbaldry*. Several of his spellings tend to be phonetic; or, to put it another way, they do not conform to the more etymological pattern that finally became fixed. Among these are *ambergrease, apostrophy, opake, ragoo* (for *ragout*) and *coopee* (for *coupe*) 'a step in dancing', anglicizations which appear also in some of his contemporaries, *dipthong* and *opthalmic*, both of which represent older forms, and recognize a more realistic pronunciation than that given in modern dictionaries. Nevertheless, as we have already noted (p. 13), *diphthong* is the spelling in the *Grammar*.

Up to now we have been considering spelling as it is in the printed book, subject, that is, to the practice, conventions, whims, and even errors of the printer. When we come to the writer's own manuscript certain other factors have to be taken into account. It is no doubt true that many writers even today spell in a rough and ready way, leaving the typist and the printer to do their best or worst with it. Unless they are strong-minded, and have settled opinions on the subject, they will not resist what printers call the custom of the house.[8] In particular, the writer will save time and space, indulge in abbreviations—a kind of private shorthand. Nowadays, such abbreviations, in as far as they are systematic, are recognized signs that are merely translated, as it were, into ordinary spelling. But in the eighteenth century both pronunciation and spelling were being influenced by this habit of shortening words; so much so that Swift in the *Tatler* and Addison in the *Spectator* protested strongly against it as a corrupting force in the language. Swift notes that 'it is a difficult Matter to read modern Books and Pamphlets: where the Words are so curtailed, and varied from their original Spelling, that whoever hath been used to plain *English*, will hardly know them by Sight'. This seems something of an exaggeration; and certainly printing conventions were more fixed later in the century, by the time of Wesley. But eighteenth-century writing—in private letters and diaries, for example—abounds in examples of phonetic spelling that reflects slapdash pronunciation. Watts, however, reminds us that a conventional spelling held its own against abbreviations and corruptions of speech. He gives some curious examples:

awkward	Pr.	aurkurd or unkurd
balluster	Pr.	bannister
atchievement	Pr.	hatchment
apprentice	Pr.	prentis
apothecary	Pr.	potticary
anemone	Pr.	emmeny
exchange	Pr.	change
exchequer	Pr.	checker

But in the end spelling won. The dictionary makers, of whom Wesley was one and Johnson the greatest, by fixing a basically 'etymological' spelling curbed the threatened corruption of the language by loose and slipshod pro-

[8] For a note on this subject see my *Spelling* (André Deutsch, 1954).

nunciation. Swift's fears for orthography proved to be unfounded; nevertheless between pronunciation and spelling discrepancies remained, and remain to this day.

Any study of the system of shorthand, based partly on John Byrom's,[9] which Wesley used extensively in the *Journal*, is outside the scope of this book. But some of the earlier *Journal* entries are written in an abbreviated language that has an interest of its own. Here are two passages that belong to his time in Georgia:

Wedn. Oct. 13 [1736]. I set out for Frederica and came thither early on Sat. morn ye 16. I met Mark Hird on ye Bluff, w^o gave me a melancholy acc^t of ye State of things there. The Publick Service had been long discontinued; & from y^t time everything was grown worse & worse. Mr Tackner had thrown off ye Form as well as ye Power of Godliness, & so had most of his neighbours, who had ever any pretensions to it.

Even poor Miss Sophy was scarce ye Shadow of w^t She was w^n I left her. I endeavourd to   her of it; but in vain. And to put it effectually out of my power so to do, She was resolvd to return to England immediately. I was at first a little surprizd, but I soon recollected my Spirits, and rememberd my Calling. 'Greater is He y^t is in you, y^n he y^t is in ye World.'

1737. Tu. Aug. 9. I was apprehended by virtue of a Warrant from ye Recorder & carried before ye Magistrates. Mr Williamson's Charge agst me was 1. y^t I had defamed his Wife, 2. y^t I had causelessly repeld her from ye H. Comu^n. The first Article I denied: as to ye 2^d, being purely Ecclesiastical, i c^d not acknowledge their Power to interrogate me.

One or two points deserve comment. What may be termed demonstrative (*th-*) and relative (*wh-*) words are systematically abbreviated. The *th* is represented by *y*, a corrupted form of the Old English thorn (þ) in y^e (*the*), y^t (*that*), and y^n (*then*), the vowel being omitted when a consonant followed; so *wh* is plain *w* in w^o (*who*) and, the vowel omitted, in w^n (*when*) and w^t (*what*). A few other words—acc^t, agst, Comu^n, c^d—are *ad hoc* and

[9] Author of 'Christians awake! salute the happy morn'.

clearly intelligible abbreviations. Such forms are common in all eighteenth-century intimate writing—in Gray's letters, for example; they have no special significance in spelling generally. More significant is Wesley's omission of the mute *e* from the verbal suffix *-ed* in *endeavourd, resolvd, surprizd, rememberd,* and *repeld*. This convention had drawn forth specific protests from Swift, who objected to the leaving out of a vowel 'to save a syllable', as in *drudg'd, disturb'd, rebuk'd, fledg'd,* and Addison, who, giving for examples *drown'd, walk'd, arriv'd,* declared that such abbreviations 'turned a tenth part of our sloothest words into so many clusters of consonants'. Their argument is, it must be confessed, difficult to follow if the *e* was already, or already becoming, mute in pronunciation. They seem, indeed, to be arguing from the appearance of the words to the eye rather than from the sound, though no doubt the *e*, and therefore the syllable, was still frequently pronounced in ordinary speech. But Wesley went farther than Swift or Addison, and left out the apostrophe; that is, he did not recognize the omission of the *e* as a conventional abbreviation but as an integral part of the spelling. Many such forms appear in his letters, though not with any consistency, unless we make the difficult assumption that where he retains the *e* it was actually sounded. To take but one example. In the draft of his famous letter to William Law, printed in facsimile in Telford's *Life*, he writes *preachd, advisd, publishd, discernd, explaind,* but also *advis'd, advised, discern'd,* and *adhered*. In the *Hymns* (1780) such forms as *fixt, incompast, mixt,* and *stampt* appear where the -(*e*)*d* is phonetically hard (=t), as, in fact, they did in other writers of the period, and do in some later poets, especially Tennyson and Bridges. The convention, such as it is, is evidently (like others at this period) a loose one. All that can be said is that on the whole Wesley is not afraid to follow the sound (or lack of it) in the spelling even if 'clusters of consonants' offend the fastidious eye.

It is in verse that the apostrophe for the mute *e*, not only in the past forms of verbs, is most familiar to us, no doubt because the poets desired to avoid any ambiguity that would affect the metrical scansion:

> *Th' embroider'd King who shows but half his face,*
> *And his refulgent Queen, with pow'rs combin'd*
> *Of broken troops an easy conquest find.*

And here a convention in the printing of the 1780 *Collection of Hymns* is of special interest: the mute *e*s appear but with a kind of inverted apostrophe over them. Two short passages from a familiar hymn will illustrate this:

> *But meet the sons of night,*
>   *But mock their vain design,*
> *Armèd in the arms of heavènly light,*
>   *Of righteòusness divine.*
>
> *Take evèry virtue, evèry grace,*
>   *And fortify the whole;*
> *Indissolubly joinèd,*
>   *To battle all proceed . . .*

On the whole, this marking is consistent, though one or two curious points arise. We have already seen (p. 40) that where the third edition has *entèrance* the first has *entrance* in the modern style. The spelling of such words, in which the *e* was so lightly stressed in ordinary speech as to be mute, took some time to settle down even after the publication of Johnson's *Dictionary*. Wesley, for example, has *doggrel* in the *Dictionary* but *doggerel* in the Preface to the 1780 *Hymns*. It is evident from the mark over the *e* in *righteousness* in the above quotation that the word was sometimes given four syllables, as indeed it still is by some who reserve a special pronunciation for the pulpit. Now and then the marking is a little baffling. For example, *righteous* would seem to require the elision of the syllable in the lines:

> *That full, divine conformity*
>   *To all my Saviour's righteous will,*

but there is no mark to indicate it. In the third edition, there is even a mark over the *e* in *duteous:*

> *Jesu, whose glory's streaming rays,*
> *Though dutèous to thy high command.*

But that may be a mere misprint, as the first edition has plain *duteous*. If not, we are left with a puzzle in pronunciation—*dutous* or *dushous? Plenteous* presents the same problem. However, in these words the *e* is so lightly sounded as to make no difference either way. More surprising is the elision in *strugglest*:

> *In vain thou strugglèst to get free,*
> *I never will unloose my hold.*

There Addison's complaint about 'clusters of consonants' would seem to be justified.

The ordinary apostrophe has one or two rather odd uses. It indicates the omission of consonants (as in *o'er*) and vowels other than mute *e*—notably in the word *toward:*

> *We worship tow'rd that holy place.*

But what pronunciation exactly that spelling indicates it is difficult to say. More strangely, it is sometimes a separator of vowels, as in *to' atone;* but even here where the elided vowel happens to be an *e* it is placed not after but above it:

> *Wè are marching through Immanuel's ground.*

In pronoun possessives, as we have already seen, it tends to come and go; but in *its*, strangely enough, the apostrophe is usual (*it's*). Wesley also, like other contemporary writers, commonly uses such abbreviations as *thro'* and *tho'*, and in his letters pretty consistently writes *shou'd* and *wou'd*.

The use of capital letters for common nouns was common in eighteenth-century writing and printing. Watts says (1734) in a section called 'Of Great Letters' that 'it has been the growing Custom of this Age in

JOHN WESLEY'S *DICTIONARY* 47

printing of every thing, but especially Poetry and Verse, to begin every Name of a thing (which is called a Noun Substantive) with a Great Letter; tho' I cannot approve it so universally as it is practised'. His own usage illustrates in some degree the custom of which he mildly disapproves. In Wesley's practice—as indeed in that of contemporary writers—it is difficult to trace any consistency at all. One or two comments, however, may be profitable. Early editions of the printed *Works* abound, as we should expect, in capitals which do not appear in modern reprints. Here, by way of example, is a short passage from the *Journal* (23rd September 1755), first as it is printed in the Standard (Curnock's) edition of 1938, and then as it stands in the edition of 1761, printed by William Pine, of Bistol:

Tues. 23.—We walked up to Glastonbury Tower, which a gentleman is now repairing. It is the steeple of a church, the foundation of which is still discernible. On the west side of the tower there are niches for images, one of which, as big as the life, is still entire. The hill on which it stands is extremely steep, and of an uncommon height; so that it commands the country on all sides, as well as the Bristol Channel. I was weary enough when we came to Bristol, but I preached till all my complaints were gone, and I had now a little leisure to sit still, and finish the *Notes on the New Testament*.

Tues. 23.—We walked up to Glastonbury-Tower, which a gentleman is repairing. It is the steeple of a Church, the Foundation of which is still discernible. On the West Side of the Tower there are Niches for Images; one of which, as big as the Life, is still entire. The Hill on which it stands is extremely steep, and of an uncommon Height; so that it commands the Country on all Sides, as well as the Bristol Channel. I was weary enough when we came to Bristol. But I preached till all my Complaints were gone; and I had now a little Leisure to sit still, and finish the *Notes on the Testament*.

That does not prove much, since we are looking at Wesley plain, but distorted a little, it may be, by printers' conventions. If, however, we go to an actual manuscript we are led to the conclusion that this kind of capitalization was by no means systematic. To take but one example. In a letter written to Lady Maxwell (7th May 1767—Telford, Vol. V, p. 47), there are, up to the last two or three sentences that precede which is, of course, printed according to modern conventions, the subscription, only seven capitalized common nouns (excluding those, of course, which begin a sentence) out of some thirty-three. There seems to be a tendency to begin abstract nouns with a capital (Correspondence, Affection, Trial, Happiness, Spirit, Weakness), yet, of these, two (*trial* and *spirit*) appear also without a capital. But when we come to the final sentences capitals increase:

> I shall hope to receive a particular Account of your Health, and of your present situation in all respects. Need there be any Reserve between Us? Cannot you speak to me with all simplicity? May the Peace and Love of GOD fill and rule your Heart!

We can only conclude that at this period, and certainly in Wesley, capitalization was, to echo Sam Weller again, a matter dependent upon the taste and fancy of the writer.

In view of Watts's statement that 'great letters' appear 'especially in poetry and verse'—which is true, as we realize when we read, say, *The Rape of the Lock* or *The Vanity of Human Wishes* in the original text—it is strange that common nouns are not capitalized in the hymns of the 1780 *Collection*.[10] There are several examples in the *Preface*, some of which are retained in the reprint (a curious example of editorial carelessness if the text was intended to represent the original) given in the present Hymn-book. But the hymns themselves rarely exhibit any departures, in this respect, from modern conventions—except, indeed, that pronouns relating to God and the Lord Jesus Christ are not printed with capitals. But here the practice

---

[10] The 1780 *Collection* of Hymns is included, since though most of the hymns are Charles's, it is reasonable to suppose that John, as editor, was responsible for the printed book as we have it.

JOHN WESLEY'S *DICTIONARY*

follows that of the early Prayer Books and the Authorized Version (1611).

So much, then, for the outward forms in Wesley, as exemplified in the *Dictionary* itself and in certain of his familiar works. In the following chapter a similar study, based mainly on the *Journal*, is made of his syntax and style.

III

The Syntax of John Wesley's *Journal*

SINCE ENGLISH is a living language, the literary usage of the eighteenth century differs somewhat from our own. The difference is not marked or obvious; it reveals itself in little details of construction, syntactical idiom, vocabulary, and punctuation. Whether we read, for example, *Gulliver's Travels*, Boswell's *Johnson*, Johnson's *Lives of the Poets*, or Cowper's *Letters* we are conscious of it. It has nothing to do with that indefinable something in writing that we call style, but rather with what C. E. Montague in *A Writer's Notes on His Trade* termed the 'mechanics of English'. In two hundred years the principles of usage, even the rules of 'grammar', such as they are, have changed a little. What was accepted then is not accepted now. Certain turns of expression have fallen out of use; grammatical constructions unquestioned then are now questionable and often condemned; some words have become obsolescent or obsolete, others have changed their meaning and, with it, their construction in relation to other words; the conventions governing the use of points and marks, as Cobbett has it, have been affected at different times by changes of fashion. In short, we cannot judge the mechanics of eighteenth-century English—or, indeed, of any English of the past—by the mechanics of our own.

Wesley's works are voluminous, but only one book or series of books, the *Journal*, belongs in any ordinary sense to literature; so it is on the prose of the *Journal* that the comments in this chapter are based. We may say at the outset, without fear of contradiction, that Wesley's English is singularly pure—it conforms, that is, to the literary usage of his day. Of his general style something will be said later on; syntactically, he is, judged by the grammatical principles of the mid-eighteenth century, almost if not quite beyond reproach.

It is interesting to note how certain constructions now frowned upon by grammarians and writers on usage occur quite commonly in older authors. One of these is what is now called the mis-related or unrelated participle phrase. It is significant that Cobbett, as fierce a critic of other men's English as of their politics, does not mention it in his *Grammar*, and indeed has no scruples about using it himself in the text. But later grammarians—notably Fowler and Partidge in our own day—possessed with a passion for a logical construction of the sentence, have declared that the participle phrase, being adjectival in function, must be so placed in the sentence that by its position it unambiguously qualifies the noun or pronoun it is intended to qualify. A simple example will make this clear. In the sentence '*Sitting on the gate*, I watched the aeroplane circle above me' the participle phrase (italicized) is logically related to its pronoun (*I*); in the sentence '*Sitting on the gate*, the aeroplane circled above me' there is only a general, not a grammatically logical, relationship —that is, the phrase by its position is associated with an inappropriate noun (*aeroplane*). This loose construction is quite common in Wesley, as it is, for example, in Addison. Here are a few examples:

Being Easter-day, I preached in our college chapel (2nd April 1738).

Seeing many of the rich at Clifton Church, my heart was much pained for them (20th May 1739).

Missing our passage over the Severn in the morning, it was sunset before we could get to Newport (1st October 1741).

Falling on the edge of one of them [the steps], it broke the case of an almanack, which was in my pocket, all to pieces (13th August 1779).

He uses also, though less frequently, the loose construction with the verb-noun form in *-ing* after a preposition in an adverb phrase:

After preaching, one of the bailies of the town came to me (25th April 1751).

By applying treacle twice a day, all the soreness was removed (18th December 1765).

In all these sentences there is now what we regard as a faulty grammatical relationship. It would seem from the first sentence that one of the bailies has been preaching, not Wesley. Nevertheless, they are evidence, not of carelessness on the part of Wesley, but of a freedom of construction that once passed muster, and now, though still in fact common in actual usage, offends against usage as grammarians think it ought to be.

One or two of his other constructions with the *-ing* form of the verb are interesting. He is fond of the absolute phrase, which, though sometimes foolishly condemned as a Latinism,[1] has had its place in English since the time of King Alfred, and plays an important part in our sentence structure. In particular, he uses it at the beginning of a sentence, to indicate the reason for the action described in the main sentence:

The wind being contrary, we did not reach Port-Royal till Wednesday evening (26th July 1736).

My horse tiring, I was obliged to return the straight way to Charlestown (2nd August 1736).

The wind being east, I was pleasing myself that we should have it on our back (6th March 1758).

and (in a longer, more sustained phrase)

The minister of Gratton sending me word I was welcome to the use of his church, I ordered notice to be given that the service would begin there at six o'clock (15th March 1779).

[1] Following the Latin ablative absolute: '*Urbe capto*, Caesar profectus est', '*The city being taken*, Caesar set forth'.

In the following brief passage there are no fewer than three examples:

So I preached in the street, both this evening, and at five on Tuesday morning; *the moon giving us as much light as we wanted*, till the sun supplied her place. I then returned to Cork. On Friday the 6th *the ship being under sail*, we took boat, and came to Cove in the evening. *All the inns being full*, we lodged at a private house (2nd October 1752).

And the following sentence is rounded off with two absolutes (both containing not the present but the past participle) which have a fine cumulative effect:

Only one [ship] got into the harbour, but grievously shattered, her rigging torn in pieces, and her main-mast gone by the board (10th October 1752).

Wesley's addiction to this construction is something of an idiosyncrasy in his syntactical style. But only occasionally —as in the passage already quoted—does it obtrude itself. More often it adds a certain elegance, or even vividness, to the sentence, as indeed it does in any writing where it is used with discretion.

One older construction, now obsolete, occurs frequently in the earlier sections of the *Journal*. This is the use of *the* before the verbal noun or gerund in *-ing*, as in the following passages:

Believing the denying ourselves, even in the smallest instances, might be helpful to us . . . (20th October 1735).

Not finding, as yet, any door open for the pursuing our main design . . .

My answer to them was that the giving or refusing the Lord's supper being a matter purely ecclesiastical . . . 9th August 1737).

. . . the hindering this, which was one of their designs was utterly disappointed (12th February 1748).

What end does the heaping them thus together answer but the gratifying an idle curiosity? (22nd October 1748).

Here the common modern idiom would demand the insertion of the preposition *of* after the *-ing* when it has a direct object. Thus the fifth sentence would read:

What end does the heaping of them thus together answer but the gratifying of an idle curiosity?

In modern English we tend, where possible, to substitute for the verbal noun in *-ing* an abstract noun—*pursuit* for *pursuing* in the second sentence, and *gratification* for *gratifying* in the fifth. We may also, even when the *-ing* form is transitive, leave it to stand by itself, without *the* and *of:* 'any time for pursuing our main design'. When it is intransitive, as in the last sentence, this construction is the normal one: 'And I hoped conversing with these holy men would be a means of establishing my soul,' though here, too, we should probably substitute the abstract noun (*conversation*) for *conversing*. It is noteworthy that in the latter part of the *Journal* the use of this old idiom (*the*+*-ing*) is far less common, evidence perhaps that it was already becoming obsolescent during Wesley's lifetime.

We have seen in Chapter 1 how Wesley sometimes uses, and prescribes in the *Grammar*, certain odd forms of the past participle and tense of strong (or 'irregular') verbs. Apart from these, there are only occasional verbal expressions that deviate from modern usage. His use of the true subjunctive, for example, differs very little from our own. Even when eighteenth-century (and even modern) idiom would prefer the subjunctive, he tends to stick to the indicative form:

... speaking to none concerning the things of God, unless my heart *was* free to it ...

Now and then, again in the early part of the *Journal*, an older idiom crops up:

I asked one of them afterwards, 'Was you not afraid?' (25th January 1736).

'... who *was* escaped thence with the skin of his teeth' (22nd December 1737).

But several *were* got to our inn before me (30th May 1742).

The wind *was* turned full north (15th February 1747).

And he occasionally uses a negative tense without the auxiliary *do*, especially with the verb *know*—'How to get on he knew not, as he had no money.' This, however, may well be a lingering and unconscious reminiscence of the prose of the Authorized Version.

We have already seen (p. 17) that in the earlier part of the century there was some doubt about the forms of the relative pronoun. On the whole, Wesley's usage in the *Journal* and elsewhere conforms, except in a matter of punctuation, which is discussed later, with our own— that is, he uses *who, whom, whose, which, that,* very much as would a modern writer. However, odd constructions crop up occasionally. Two will suffice as examples:

Our aim was . . . to keep them from want and idleness, in order to which we took twelve of the poorest and a teacher into the society-room (25th November 1740).

Here there is a kind of elliptical construction with the compound 'in order to', which in modern standard English is always followed by the verb infinitive—that is, 'in order to' represents the *to* of the normal infinitive phrase when purpose is suggested. Here we should insert the verb *do* before *which*, and probably omit 'in order'; or, more idiomatically, should use the demonstrative in some such phrase as 'to do this' or 'with a view to this'. For neatness and conciseness the older construction, now lost, has much to recommend it.

Yet as I stood on a high wall, and kept my eyes upon them many were softened and grew calmer and calmer; which some of their champions observing, went round and suddenly pushed me down (7th July 1745).

This older relative construction is difficult to define;

but the general effect is that of an absolute phrase. We have it in the Authorized Version:

> We had much work to come by the boat: which when they had taken up, they used helps, undergirding the ship (Acts 27[16-17]).

and in a familiar passage of Bunyan:

> And after that they shut up the gates; which when I had seen, I wished myself among them.

Modern idiom demands the looser and more cumbrous construction *and—this* or *it*—'and when some of their champions observed this', 'and when they had taken it up', 'and when I saw this'. It is noteworthy, by the way, that—perhaps because he was using a construction already obsolescent—Wesley for once falls into syntactical error. Having boxed up his subject in the absolute *which* phrase, he should have represented it as a pronoun (*they*) in the main sentence.

It is clearly impossible to give more than a few representative examples from the *Journal* of Wesley's use of words with a meaning, and sometimes a syntactical construction, that has now become obsolescent or obsolete. Sometimes the usage is obviously archaic, as *conclude* for *include* in the following sentence:

> I told them plainly, the Scripture had concluded them all under sin (5th June 1739).

In the *Dictionary* the word is given its modern meaning only, 'to end, to gather by reason, resolve'. More often the word concerned has an older, more truly etymological sense that is familiar to us in the work of pre-eighteenth-century writers. Thus he uses the word *want* with the 'negative' meaning 'lack' or 'be short of':

> When we wanted a league of shore it fell calm again (15th April 1749).

> I began preaching at the same hour, winter and summer, and never wanted a congregation (5th April 1784).

But this usage is only occasional; the modern 'positive' sense, 'desire', 'long for' was well established in Wesley's time, and is common in his writing. Sometimes in the hymns we may postulate a kind of transitional sense.

I want a principle within

means both 'I lack' and 'I desire'—the second meaning is a kind of overtone to the first. The modern writer, seeking for a monosyllable here would substitute, according to his intention, either 'lack' or 'seek'.

One or two Latin derivatives keep the flavour of Milton or Shakespeare—they were at this time passing from their true etymological to a popular anglicized sense. When he writes 'Which, then, shall we most admire, the ignorance or confidence of those that affirm population decreases in England?' he is using *admire* as Milton used it in 'Let none admire that riches grow in hell'—that is, as a synonym for 'wonder at', not for 'regard with pleased surprise or approval' (*Concise Oxford Dictionary*). To us, familiar with the modern restricted sense of *disappoint*, which always implies the loss of something good or desirable, the following sentence seems a little strange:

I expected little good here: but I was happily disappointed (24th October 1749).

or, in this, from his description of the opening of City Road chapel:

Many were afraid that the multitudes, crowding from all parts, would have occasioned much disturbance. But they were happily disappointed (1st November 1778).

But *disappoint*, as we know from older writers, originally had a wider meaning that allowed its association with evil or sorrow as well as good. We still keep the idiom, though not commonly, in such an expression as 'I was agreeably disappointed'. *Prevent*, whose older etymological sense ('come or go before') we know from the Prayer Book ('Prevent us, O Lord, in all our doings'), Wesley normally uses with its modern meaning in prose:

'If but one of them had struck him it would have prevented him from driving any farther.' But the older sense occasionally occurs in the *Hymns* (1780):

> *Thy eyes must all my thoughts survey,*
> *Preventing what my lips would say,*

where *preventing* means *anticipating*. It is, oddly enough, this meaning which he gives in the *Dictionary:* 'to come or go before'. In one sentence he has a peculiar use of the word *exquisite*, as well as the older sense of *admire:* 'I admired the exquisite stupidity of the people' (30th July 1770). For *exquisite* the *Dictionary* has 'rare, choice, excellent'. Perhaps *rare* would suit the context here, though *intense* is nearer the meaning, as we still use it in 'exquisite joy', 'exquisite torture'. He also uses *ludicrous* in the active ('laughing', 'ribald') instead of the modern passive ('laughable') sense: 'A few of the hearers were a little ludicrous at first; but their mirth was quickly spoiled' (21st May 1764). The *Oxford English Dictionary* notes this sense as becoming obsolete in 1780. Wesley himself has 'sporting, trifling, merry'.

Now and then a word reminds us of the circumstances of his age—a little before the Industrial Revolution. On 1st April 1754 he started off, with his wife, from Bristol. 'We set out', he says, 'in the machine, and the next evening reached the Foundery.' The machine was, of course, a kind of coach; and the word was only just then moving into its modern association with cogs, and wheels, and factories. For what we should call his electric *machine* Wesley himself uses the term *apparatus*—a hint, perhaps, that *machine* was then in a transitional stage of meaning. However that may be, he once, perhaps remembering Hamlet,[2] refers to the body as a machine: 'O, how imperfectly do we understand even the machine which we carry about with us!' (3rd July 1764). Oddly enough, Wesley's sense survives, a little precariously, with reference to a bicycle. *Apparatus*, by the way, he defines a

[2] In his letter to Ophelia, 'While this machine is to him'.

SYNTAX OF THE *JOURNAL* 59

trifle cryptically as 'preparation for, tools, furniture'. Another word of the same type is *engine*, in those pre-railway days keeping its wide and etymological sense of 'contrivance', 'anything made by *ingenuity*', or, as Wesley himself has it, 'an instrument to effect anything'. One of the passages in which Wesley uses it has a certain vividness and gentle humour. He had come (25th May 1752) to Barnard Castle, where he attempted to preach to a mob of noisy people, only a few of whom could hear, but who, however, 'listened with huge attention'. 'To prevent this', he says, 'some of the rabble fetched the engine, and threw a good deal of water on the congregation; but not a drop fell on me.' But this, as it happens, does not prove much; for a contrivance that squirts water is still called a fire-engine.

Wesley always uses the adverb *presently* in its original etymological sense, 'immediately', 'there and then'; the modern rather puzzling change of meaning to 'in a short, vaguely defined, time' did not establish itself until the nineteenth century. 'The north wind', he says, 'being unusually high, drove the sleet in our face, which froze as it fell, and cased us over presently' (1st April 1753). He also uses the word with *after*, as we still use *immediately:* 'Presently after he went, my mare stuck fast in a quagmire' (15th April 1753). It is remarkable that in the Standard (Curnock's) Edition of the *Journal* a comma after *presently* obscures the true meaning.

Now and then, but not as often as we should like, Wesley comments on a word. In the entry for 15th April 1772 he recounts an interesting little anecdote. 'Here [Selkirk] I observed', he said, 'a little piece of stateliness which was quite near to me: the maid came in, and said, "Sir, the lord of the stable wants to know if he should feed your horses." We call him ostler in England.' He does not add (and probably did not know) that the humble origin of the word *lord*, 'the loaf guardian', might well explain this little piece of stateliness.[3] On another

[3] O.E. *hlaford* from *hlaf*, 'loaf', and *weard*, 'ward', 'guardian'.

occasion (9th June 1742) he sheds light, by implication, on the pronunciation of a word: 'Yes, sir', said an old man; 'an't please your worship, they have *convarted* my wife.' This opens up the whole fascinating subject of eighteenth-century pronunciation—one which is outside the scope and intention of this book. It is sufficient to say, on this particular point, that the broadening of the vowel before *r*, surviving still in some words, as for example *clerk* and *Derby*, was very common in the eighteenth century, among all classes, and was reflected in such spellings as *sarvant* and *vardict*. The modern abbreviation *Varsity* gives a hint as to its loftier connexions. But, more generally, this passing comment of Wesley's reminds us that in his journeyings he must have made a wide acquaintance with, and as a linguist himself been keenly interested in, the dialect words, the queer pronunciations, and the queerer spellings that characterized the period. This whole subject is dealt with in a fascinating chapter in J. H. Whiteley's *Wesley's England*,[4] to which the reader is referred. But of this other popular language, as we may call it, the *Journal* bears little trace. Wesley, himself a scholar, wrote in the 'literary' idiom of his day—the English which even then, in its general syntax and outward forms, was being in some sense, though not completely or finally, standardized.

But perhaps his most interesting commentary on an individual word occurs in the entry for 11th February 1772:

I casually took a volume of what is called 'A Sentimental Journey through France and Italy'. Sentimental! what is that? It is not English: he might as well say, Continental. It is not sense. It conveys no determinate idea; yet one fool makes many. And this nonsensical word (who would believe it?) is become a fashionable one! However, the book agrees full well with the title; for one is as queer as the other. For oddity, uncouthness, and unlikeness to all the world beside, I suppose, the writer is without a rival.

[4] Epworth Press (1938).

It is not surprising that Wesley had been bewildered and angered by Sterne. But his objection to a new term (like many of those which are advanced in our own times) has been overruled in the natural development of the language. *A Sentimental Journey* was published four years before Wesley read it, and no doubt it helped to popularize a word that was just then gaining a footing in English. The truth is that in the second half of the century the age of 'reason' was giving way to what may be called an age of 'feeling'. In 1762 Rousseau—of whom Wesley said 'Sure a more consummate coxcomb never saw the sun!' —had published *Emile*, with the sub-title *L'Education Sentimentale*. Wesley's complaint that the word 'conveys no determinate idea' is not entirely beside the mark. To this day the derivatives of the Latin *sentio*, 'feel', have in English a certain haziness of meaning, or at any rate are not easily or sharply definable. Wesley himself (like most of the eighteenth-century writers) uses *sensible* as we use *sensitive*: 'I preached in the morning at Newport . . . to the most insensible, ill-behaved people I have ever seen in Wales' (19th October 1739). So, too, in the 1780 *Hymns:*

> Saviour, to me in pity give
> The sensible distress.

The noun *sensibility* (a little later to be used by Jane Austen in a title which also reflects the 'feeling' of the period) still retains this meaning. But *sensibility, sensitiveness, sentiment,* and *sentimentality* are words that still give a writer pause, and tax the powers of the lexicographer. In the *Dictionary* Wesley himself has only three words from the *sentis* root:

a sensation,   perception by sense
sensitive,   having sense
sensuality,   indulging the senses, voluptuousness

It is true to say that in the *Journal* Wesley's idiom is in the best sense 'literary'. He did not write in what Southey called the 'home-spun' of Bunyan. But his language and syntactical patterns are never merely academic; they bear abundant evidence of the impact of common speech. His sentences move without creaking—except, perhaps, in those constructions already noticed (pp. 51-6) which are now obsolete. Dryden's superstition about the preposition at the end of the sentence had long been exploded as a fallacy. Certainly Wesley had no inhibitions: 'I saw only one or two who behaved lightly, whom I immediately spoke to.' So, too, he regularly omits the relative pronoun in the oblique case—'as I did next day to a young man I overtook on the road'; and sometimes almost irregularly omits the conjunction in a dependent clause: 'Believing one hindrance of the work of God in York was the neglect of field preaching,' 'Many would wonder we would still stay without the walls,' 'They wondered what was the matter I did not rise.'

Now and then, but not often, his use of prepositions does not agree with our own. He writes, for example, 'exasperated against', 'on the green adjoining to the castle', 'not to act independently on each other'. But this has no special significance, since prepositional usage crystallized only with the more or less dogmatic pronouncements of grammarians after Wesley's time.

From time to time older syntactical idioms appear: 'being to leave the town next morning', 'the key not being to be found', 'Some advised me to go another place; but I knew it needed not,' 'unless my heart was free to it'. He does not hesitate at a construction which even now causes the purists to raise their eyebrows: 'But the congregation, as well as me, had something else to think of.' Thus does an eighteenth-century freedom reprove a modern finnickiness and adherence to mere grammatical superstition.

He frequently has an adjective where we should today use an adverb form—a reflection of an older custom based on colloquial speech: 'The church was so excessive hot,' 'It is scarce possible,' 'a huge rock rising perpendicular from the sea'. Older adverb and prepositional uses occur occasionally—for example, *without* for 'outside' ('without Lawford's gate'), and *abroad* for 'in the open' ('It was too cold for them to stand abroad.') Such former adverbial connectives as *wherewith, wherein, therewith, therefrom* are common. They were about that time beginning to give way to our modern phrasal equivalents, in which we use the preposition before a relative or demonstrative pronoun ('in which' 'from this'), and have in Wesley's prose a faintly archaic air.

Wesley by no means eschews the kind of figurative language that is itself a vital part of English idiom. Of this his most famous sentence 'I felt my heart strangely warmed' is sufficient example. But his pages are not, like Bunyan's, studded with homely and colloquial expressions direct from the conversation of ordinary men. Nevertheless, such expressions do sometimes occur. 'All the quarrels', he writes (17th June 1736), 'that have been here since you came have been 'long of you.' That is patently colloquial. Others, like 'I wrote a line to him immediately' and 'a sermon quite innocent of meaning' are more literary. Some, direct and vivid enough, have not survived—'By the time we had gone a mile beyond it, we were out of all path,' 'and one of them stole off his hat', 'They were at a stand again,' 'They made no more stop.' And occasionally, when his feelings run high, he allowed himself an unusually forceful piece of imagery— 'They that can believe this, may believe a man's getting into a bottle.'

Thus far we have thought of Wesley's prose in relation to the conventions and syntactical patterns of his age; and have done no more than establish the fact that it reflects the idiom—often since amended and changed— of the eighteenth century. It is now time to consider one or two of his individual characteristics. The first, from which the others directly or remotely derive, is his addiction to direct speech. This gives his narrative, as it does Boswell's and to some extent Bunyan's, a forthright vividness:

As soon as I was in the midst of them, I called for a chair; and standing up, asked, 'What do any of you want with me?' Some said, 'We want you to go with us to the justice.' I replied, 'That I will, with all my heart.' I then spoke a few words, which God applied; so that they cried out, with might and main, 'The gentleman is an honest gentleman, and we will spill our blood in his defence.' I asked, 'Shall we go to the justice tonight, or in the morning?' Most of them cried, 'Tonight, tonight'; on which I went before, and two or three hundred followed; the rest returning whence they came.

There is a more familiar example in his account of his encounter with Beau Nash, where he drops at the outset into pure dialogue, without any connectives:

'Sir, did you ever hear me preach?' 'No.' 'How, then, can you judge of what you never heard?' 'Sir, by common report.' 'Common report is not enough. Give me leave, Sir, to ask. "Is not your name Nash?"' 'My name is Nash.' 'Sir, I dare not judge of you by common report: I think it not enough to judge by.' Here he paused awhile, and, having recovered himself, said, 'I desire to know what this people comes here for': on which one replied, 'Sir, leave him to me: let an old woman answer him. You, Mr Nash, take care of your body; we take care of our souls; and for the food of our souls we come here.' He replied not a word, but walked away.

The advantages of this device for the presentation of a living picture are obvious, especially if we venture on the exercise of reducing the passages to indirect speech. There is only one slight disadvantage—a certain jerkiness in the sentences, as if the writer pauses momentarily at intervals, and then goes on again. To put it another way, the narrative in indirect speech would gain in smoothness what it would lack in vividness and realism. This momentary pause is most noticeable in Wesley's use of the direct question. There is an example of it in the Beau Nash story quoted above: 'Give me leave, Sir, to ask, "Is not your name Nash?"'.' Here, as in other recorded dialogue, we may assume that the direct question faithfully represents the words actually spoken. But in ordinary narrative he often follows what was then a fairly common convention; that is, he promises what would be in modern English an indirect question, but pauses and makes it direct:

I afterwards asked him, what he expected when the mob came upon us?

and without the question mark, but with the direct construction,

I consulted my friends, whether God did not call me to return to England.

But he goes farther, and uses the direct question in an individual way:

The point on which we desired all the preachers to speak their minds at large was, 'Whether we ought to separate from the Church?'

Sometimes, too, he makes a statement by using the device of question and answer:

If it was said, 'But did not the trustees of Georgia appoint you to be minister of Savannah?' I replied, 'They did; but it was not done by my solicitation; it was done without either my desire or knowledge.'

So, on his eighty-fifth birthday he sets out the reasons for his long life in a series of questions:

May we not impute it as inferior means,[5]
1. To my constant exercise and change of air?
2. To my never having lost a night's sleep, sick or well, at land or at sea, since I was born?
3. To my having sleep at command; so that whenever I feel myself almost worn out, I call it, and it comes, day or night?
4. To my having constantly, for above sixty years, risen at four in the morning?
5. To my constant preaching at five in the morning, for above fifty years?
6. To my having had so little pain in my life; and so little sorrow, or anxious care?

[5] That is, inferior to the power of God and 'the prayers of his children'.

This predilection for the direct question on the part of Wesley is reflected in the official language of Methodism. Whenever the Annual Trustees' meeting is faced with the Questions relating to the state of the Trust, the shade of Wesley is there.

It is noticeable also, that Wesley is fond—too fond—of exclamations and rhetorical questions. One such, his horrified comment on Rousseau, has already been quoted (p. 61). Here are one or two other examples, taken from the entries for successive days (21st, 22nd June 1759):

A single tomb I observed there, which was about a hundred and thirty years old; but the inscription was very hardly legible. So soon do even our sepulchres die! Strange, that men should be careful about them! But are not many self-condemned therein?

How little did the late duke imagine that his son would plough up his mark, and let his house run to ruin! But let it go! In a little time the earth itself, and all the works of it, shall be burned up.

It is arguable that in these and many other similar passages the commentary would, in fact, be more effective if it were made in the indirect narrative style; that the transition from statement to exclamation or question is awkward and unnatural, as well as a little naïve. On the other hand, it lends to the prose a certain spontaneity. Wesley, meditating as he rides along on this and that, suddenly turns and challenges the reader, rhetorically, with his spoken thought. Another rider up and down England half a century afterwards had the same trick in the record of his travels. William Cobbett, like John Wesley, was a downright man; and like him, he turns on his horse to ejaculate, as it were, across the years. Wesley's *Journal* and *Rural Rides* have much in common, and not least this tendency of their writers to break off their narrative in moments of personal emotion, and stir the reader into sharing their own surprise, or delight, or indignation.

Parallel with Wesley's addiction to the direct question is

SYNTAX OF THE *JOURNAL* 67

his habit of summarizing his argument and conclusions in numbered clauses or sentences. This is, perhaps, his most obvious idiosyncrasy; one, too, that betrays the methodistical mind. Perhaps his mother's 'by-laws', which he records in detail in his entry on the day of her funeral (1st August 1742), had induced early in his mind the value of a kind of mechanical system and order in the presentation of such facts as lent themselves to classification or logical display. It is in this manner that he records, from time to time, his own resolutions, or gives an account of the reasons for his continued health and activity:

Friday, 28th June 1782, I entered into my eightieth year; but, blessed be God, my time is not 'labour and sorrow'. I find no more pain or bodily infirmities than at five-and-twenty. This I shall impute, 1. To the power of God, fitting me for what he calls me to. 2. To my still travelling four or five thousand miles a year. 3. To my sleeping, night and day, whenever I want it. 4. To my rising at a set hour. And, 5. To my constant preaching, particularly in the morning.

Here the method of systematic enumeration is understandable; but he sometimes uses it, less naturally, to record quite general observations:

Sun. 18th August 1782. The bishop, inviting me to dinner, I could not but observe, 1. The lovely situation of the palace, covered with trees, and as rural and retired as if it was quite in the country. 2. The plainness of the furniture, not costly or showy, but just fit for a Christian bishop. 3. The dinner sufficient, but not redundant; plain and good, but not delicate. 4. The propriety of the company—five clergymen and four of the aldermen; and 5. The genuine, unaffected courtesy of the bishop.

It is interesting to speculate on the thoughts of the courteous bishop if he could have read the orderly and ordered mind of his venerable guest.

On the whole, the *Journal* has been underestimated as a piece of literature. It has never taken its place with the *Diary* of Pepys or Evelyn, with *Rural Rides*, or even some lesser journals and personal records. Wesley himself said, 'I dare no more write in a fine style than wear a fine coat.' And certainly there is no 'fine style' in his writing; indeed, in a journal this would have been out of place. But he did write, says J. H. Whiteley, 'with sterling simplicity; his prose has the muscular form and incomparable vigour with which the bulk of the people of England then spoke'. That in itself, together with the amazing story he had to tell, should have saved the *Journal* from the comparative neglect into which it has fallen among literary critics and indeed ordinary readers.

To this there is one thing to add: that, having an observant eye, he was much addicted to descriptive adjectives and adverbs. He had an observant eye for natural beauty and for people; and he often painted a scene or described his congregation with two or three carefully chosen epithets. 'At one I went to the market-place in Dudley', he writes on 24th October 1749, 'and proclaimed the name of the Lord to an huge, unwieldy, noisy multitude.' Ten years later (30th August 1759) he told the society at Norwich 'in plain terms that they were the most ignorant, self-conceited, self-willed, fickle, untractable, disorderly, disjointed society that I knew in the three kingdoms'. There is an almost Shakespearian gusto in that, a kind of crescendo of language. In depicting scenery and the various sights that caught his eye as he rode along he is gentler, sometimes almost lyrical. 'We rode on softly in a calm, moon-shiny night'—there are many brief passages such as this scattered up and down the pages, especially when a sense of the weather breaks in, as it were, upon his meditations. In this he has some kinship with Gray, in his letters, or with White of Selborne. The short passage about the watch-night service, quoted on p. 34, is a good example of his general descriptive style, which does not rely on the piling up of epithets but on an easy if somewhat formal simplicity. There are many others like it in the *Journal*. Fine writing was, as he says, alien to him. But he had what was better, a natural feeling for words, and a sense of English prose.

IV

The Language, Metre, and Rhyme of Charles Wesley's Hymns

'MANY GENTLEMEN', says John Wesley, in the Preface to the *Hymns* (1780), 'have done my Brother and me (though without naming us) the honour to reprint many of our hymns. Now they are perfectly welcome so to do, provided they print them just as they are. But I desire, they would not attempt to mend them: for really they are not able. None of them is able to mend either the sense, or the verse. Therefore I must beg of them one of these two favours: either to let them stand just as they are, to take them for better for worse: or to add the true reading in the margin, or at the bottom of the page; that we may no longer be accountable either for the nonsense, or for the doggerel of other men.' It would appear from this that he is referring to literary integrity. What he and his brother had written they had written; to tamper with it was to take an unjustifiable liberty, and, more than that, to reduce, or tend to reduce, poetry to doggerel. The principle which underlies his protest is widely recognized. A piece of literature is sacrosanct. True, the bowdlerizer sometimes, for what may even seem to be legitimate reasons, lays his hands upon it. But, however pure his motives may be, he is an intruder, a profaner of the temple. Yet hymns have always been curiously liable to the attentions of the editor; indeed, John Wesley himself did not hesitate to make minor and even major alterations in his brother's language and expression when he felt it necessary. There is a kind of convention in the matter which, since it is widely accepted, must have some reason and even justification.

And the reason is, after all, not far to seek. A hymn is primarily meant to be sung in public by a congregation of people, not read in private. For this reason there has to be sometimes (though not often) an accommodation of sound or rhythm to a musical tune. As it happens, there are two familiar examples of this in the hymns of Isaac Watts. Watts wrote:

Our God, our help in ages past,

but most modern hymn-books, though not all, accept John Wesley's emendation and change this to

O God, our help in ages past,

to avoid the awkward repetition of *our*. He also originally wrote:

When I survey the wondrous cross
Where the young Prince of glory died,

but this he afterwards altered, for rhythm's sake, to the weaker and less evocative 'On which the Prince of glory died'. Then again, some hymns, especially of Wesley, were originally far too long for singing to a repetitive tune. An outstanding example of this is *Wrestling Jacob* (Come, O Thou Traveller unknown), twelve of whose original stanzas are printed in the 1933 Hymn-book (339), though they are obligingly reduced (340) to four for convenience of singing.

But more than that. It happens that Charles Wesley, and to some extent Watts, used an imagery and a mode of expression that, rightly or wrongly, no longer commend themselves to us. They followed Saint Paul, for example, in using the word *bowels* (not *heart*) as representing the seat of the emotions. But what in the prose of the Authorized Version is acceptable seems odd and out of place in a metrical hymn. In this respect, Watts is more

LANGUAGE, METRE, RHYME OF HYMNS 71

extreme than Wesley, who never descended to the depths of Watts's almost incredible

> *Here every bowel of our God*
> *With soft compassion rolls.*

There are, however, some curious examples in the 1780 *Hymns*.

> *Still Thou journeyest where I am,*
> *And still thy bowels move*

(108, v. 3) has almost a Wattsian incongruity, and so has (145, v. 4)

> *What shall I say to move*
> *The bowels of thy love?*
> *Are they not already stirred?*

There is a milder example in *Wrestling Jacob* (138, v. 7):

> *To me, to all, thy bowels move,*
> *Thy nature, and thy name is Love,*

which in the present book (339, v. 7; 340, v. 4) has been amended to:

> *To me, to all, Thy mercies move,*
> *Thy nature and Thy name is Love.*

It was Watts, too, who perpetrated the line 'And worms have learnt to lisp Thy name', where modern editors, searching for a suitable monosyllable, have substituted, not altogether happily, *babes* (M.H.B. 6). Certainly the metaphor of the worm, though it suggests and emphasizes humility, is not acceptable to modern Methodists, and does, indeed, lend itself to a certain ludicrousness of imagery. Charles Wesley uses it quite often. It occurs, for example, in a hymn ('With glorious clouds encompast round', 124, v. 1) whose language is peculiarly majestic and beautiful:

> *Will he forsake his throne above,*
> *Himself to worms impart?*

Rather oddly, the modern amendment 'Himself to me impart', though it falters a little rhythmically since the pronoun (*me*) cannot quite bear the heavy stress, suits the personal tone of that particular verse, which ends:

> *Answer, Thou Man of grief and love,*
> *And speak it to my heart!*

No doubt Wesley's metrical ear required a noun for rhythm's sake, and he resorted to *worms;* but the balance of *me* (line 2) and *my* (line 4) gives point, and almost poignancy, to the sense. Here and there, by the way, *worm* has survived in the present book, when the image is so restricted as not to be incongruous. There is an example in Hymn 574:

> *If so poor a worm as I*
> *May to Thy great glory live,*

where the simile (not metaphor) has the effect of retaining the person (*I*) in relationship to the following line. It might also be argued that, if the verse is to be kept at all, the substitution of a suitable monosyllable for *worm* is, to say the least of it, difficult.

Rather surprisingly, even more common in eighteenth-century hymnody is the emphasis on the physical details of the crucifixion—the broken body and the blood. It was the fastidious and gentlemanly Cowper who wrote:

> *There is a fountain fill'd with blood*
> *Drawn from Emmanuel's veins,*
> *And sinners plunged beneath that flood*
> *Lose all their guilty stains;*

and the hymn has been retained in the present book. We also have Toplady's

> *Let the water and the blood,*
> *From Thy riven side which flowed,*
> *Be of sin the double cure,*
> *Cleanse me from its guilt and power.*

But while, in the greatest of Watts's hymns, we still sing

> *See from His head, His hands, His feet,*
> *Sorrow and love flow mingled down,*

where the physical reference is, it must be admitted, obscured and indirect, another verse, retained in the *English Hymnal, Songs of Praise*, and other hymn-books, has been dropped by our compilers:

> *His dying crimson, like a robe,*
> *Spreads o'er his body on the tree;*
> *Then am I dead to all the globe,*
> *And all the globe is dead to me.*

The symbolism, rather than the factual details, of the blood is woven into the texture of some of Charles Wesley's hymns. It cannot be tampered with, and our peculiar Methodist hymnody would be the poorer without it. To sacrifice 'Arise, my soul, arise' (M.H.B. 368) or 'O Love divine, what hast thou done' (M.H.B. 186) because of their imagery would be almost to deny, or at any rate to minimize, the great truths of the atonement. True, in other hymns the symbolic is overwhelmed by a literalness that for us spoils the spiritual appeal:

> *See how his back the scourgers tear,*
> *While to the bloody pillar bound!*
> *The ploughers make long furrows there,*
> *Till all his body is one wound.*

These find no place in our modern hymn-books, and it is easy to understand why. In others that survive, a 'literal' epithet has sometimes been changed for one that has a more symbolical meaning, as in the first verse of 'Weary souls that wander wide' (M.H.B. 319):

> *Sink into the cleansing flood;*
> *Rise into the life of God,*

where the original phrase was 'the purple flood' (20, v. 1). But whether such amendments are justified is a matter for argument.

A few of the 1780 hymns, now for the most part no longer used, had a rather different kind of incongruity in their retention of biblical, especially Old Testament, idiom and imagery. They are usually those which are based directly on, or deliberately echo, a scriptural passage. One illustration will suffice. It is the second verse of Hymn 143 (1780):

> *O might I hear the Turtle's voice,*
> *The cooing of thy gentle Dove!*
> *The call that bids my heart rejoice;*
> *'Arise, and come away my love!*
> *The storm is gone, the winter's o'er:*
> *Arise, for thou shalt weep no more!'*

That reminiscence of the sensuous poetic language of the Song of Solomon goes uneasily into verse—especially verse for congregational singing. And the same is true of all similar Hebrew metaphor. In other words, there are biblical expressions that cannot be properly translated into, or even adapted to the style of the English hymn. This does not mean to say, of course, that in the Wesley, and other, hymns there are not frequent echoes of the Authorized Version. There are. The incongruity arises only when vocabulary and imagery alien to the western mind are unnaturally forced into a medium that by its very nature is, in a peculiar sense, 'colloquial'.

But that term 'colloquial' must not be misunderstood. 'The hymns of the eighteenth century', says Canon Adam Fox, 'had to be written in the popular language of the day, and at no period has popular language been so simple or graceful or more happily suited to the kind of things that hymns are. . . . The typical prose of the eighteenth century was plain. . . . The best prose writers of the period tried very successfully to write much as they spoke, and the hymn writers did the same.' For the 'colloquial', therefore, we may substitute the 'popular' language. Nevertheless, though Canon Fox's argument is plausible, it is not altogether sound. For we cannot read the hymns of Charles Wesley without wondering whether they could, in fact, be understood by those who sang them first—simple, often (we may assume) illiterate people. It is, indeed, safe to say that the language of many of the Wesley hymns is beyond the understanding of Methodist congregations today.

For both John and Charles Wesley were scholars, and both displayed in their work, as in their lives, the classicism of the eighteenth century. Methodism, after all, had its ultimate origin in the University; and its earliest hymnody—that is, the hymns of the Wesleys themselves —has upon it the mark of its origin. There is no attempt at a Saxon simplicity. Far from it. Charles Wesley's hymns, especially, abound in high-sounding and sonorous Latin words. It is always a little disconcerting (and refreshing) to turn at Christmas time from the cloying archaisms and pseudo-artlessness of the carols to something which is all the more forthright and beautiful for having a Latin texture; to turn, for example, from

> *In the bleak mid-winter*
> *Frosty wind made moan;*
> *Earth stood hard as iron,*
> *Water like a stone*

to

> *Let earth and heaven combine,*
> *Angels and men agree,*
> *To praise in songs divine*
> *The incarnate Deity,*
> *Our God contracted to a span,*
> *Incomprehensibly made man.*

The very words *incarnate*, *Deity*, *contracted*, *incomprehensibly*, with their strong polysyllabic rhythm, have the effect of leading us away from the tinsel, the holly and the ivy, even the legitimate homeliness of the season, to a sense of its august and high significance.

After all, long Latin derivatives often have in themselves a beautiful sound; and Charles Wesley, especially, knew how to make the best of them—and how to adapt them to the 'flow' of a repetitive tune. He loves, for example, the polysyllabic adjective, especially when it contains liquid consonants:

> Strong, and *permanent*, and clear
>
> A pure and a *permanent* light
>
> A Stream of pure *perennial* peace
>
> Nor visit as a *transient* guest
>
> With calmly *reverential* joy
>
> The blood of sprinkling speaks and prays,
> All *prevalent* for helpless men

But not only the adjective: the noun and the verb, too, have their place:

> My faith's *integrity* maintain
>
> And lost in Thine *immensity*
>
> And bright in *effulgence* divine
>
> With all his *plenitude* of grace
>
> Out of his *plenitude* receive
> Ineffable delight
>
> A *sensibility* of sin
>
> And *emulate* the angel choir
>
> *Actuate* and fill the whole
>
> Move, and *actuate*, and guide.

Dr Henry Bett (*The Hymns of Methodism*, Ch. 4), has pointed out, with many examples, how frequently a Latin word in the hymns has its original Latin rather than its modern English significance. There is no need to go over the same ground here, except to add one example to

LANGUAGE, METRE, RHYME OF HYMNS 77

those he gives for *comfort* (='strengthen') or its derivatives:

> *Bid my quiet spirit hear*
> *Thy* comfortable *voice* (465),

and to add one which he missed:

> *Where the indubitable seal*
> *That* ascertains *the kingdom mine?* (280)

Here the word *ascertain*, derived from Latin through French, has almost the sense 'guarantees', that is, 'make it certain', as in the title of one of Swift's pamphlets, quoted on p. 10.

It is interesting to note, by the way, how sometimes, for metrical reasons, Wesley uses a longer and even in his day uncurrent form of a simple word. There are at least two examples in the present Hymn-book—

> Dispread *the victory of Thy cross* (270)

and

> *Still present with thy people, Thou*
> *Bear'st them through life's* disparted *wave* (486).

But, above all, Wesley is exceedingly—almost excessively—fond of adjectives in *-able* and *-ible*, with their corresponding adverbs. In his book *Christ's Standard Bearer* G. H. Findlay notes what is perhaps the most familiar of them all:

> *There let it for Thy glory burn*
> *With* inextinguishable *blaze* (386),

and comments upon the almost incredible, and certainly crass, stupidity of the compilers of the *BBC Hymn-book* in reducing this to

> *With ever-bright, undying blaze.*

There is another example in one of the lines quoted a page or so above, '*ineffable* delight'. Among them *unutterable* (275, 339, 565, 710) and *unspeakable* (560, 745,

F

730) are favourites, but there are many others, including *unblamable* (605), *Unsearchable*, as a designation of God (172), and, with the accent thrown back on to the first syllable, *acceptable* (590). The same type of polysyllabic adverb also occurs quite frequently, as in

> *Strength and comfort from Thy word*
> Imperceptibly *supply* (545)

and

> *To Thee* inseparably *joined*
> *Let all our spirits cleave* (721)

and, finest of all, in a stanza already quoted,

> Incomprehensibly *made man* (142).

Mr Findlay (in *God's Standard Bearer*) has an excellent chapter on the varied metres of Charles Wesley's hymns, pointing out his fondness for what he calls the 'hammerhead' of the iambic lines which have a stress or accent 'fore and aft', that is, on the first as well as the last syllable, as in 'Soldiers of Christ arise'. It is interesting to speculate on the relationship of his rhythms to tunes that were already in existence; but this is a theme that is beyond the scope of this book, and indeed beyond the knowledge of its author. We may, however, be certain that the words 'sang' themselves in Wesley's mind; and it is this very fact that makes him not only the greatest of English hymnwriters but also one of the outstanding metrical experimentalists of his time. Many poets—including Gray, Collins, and Cowper—were adopting lyrical measures that had been neglected, or unknown, during the reign of the heroic couplet in the early part of the century. The simple ballad measure, used, for example, by Gray in his light-hearted poem *The Long Story*, gave the 8.6.8.6. stanza known as common metre (C.M.), usually with two sets of rhyming lines (abab). Of this the 8.8.8.8. stanza, called long metre (L.M.) was a more sustained form, standing midway between the ballad stanza and the

LANGUAGE, METRE, RHYME OF HYMNS 79

'heroic quatrain'—that is, the stanza in rhymed iambic pentameters (abab) used by Dryden in *Annus Mirabilis*. These Charles Wesley used with fine effect, as well as the truncated short metre (6.6.8.6.), with its elongated third line.

But he went, of course, far beyond these. He uses, for example, two or three types of six-lined stanzas: one in the 6.6.6.6.8.8. measure, which builds itself up through an alternately rhyming (abab) quatrain to the climax of a rhyming couplet with the extra iambic foot, as in 'Let earth and heaven agree' (142); one in the majestic 8.8.8.8.8.8. measure, which we especially associate with him—the measure of 'And can it be that I should gain' (371), the Conversion hymn (361), and *Wrestling Jacob* (339); and one in the lighter 88.6.88.6. measure (of, for example, 'Thou great mysterious God unknown', 376), which was, unlike the others, familiar in secular verse—it is the stanza of Suckling's *Ballad upon a Wedding*, of Gray's *Ode on a Favourite Cat*, and of Christopher Smart's magnificent *Song to David*. All these move in regular iambs, except that, as already pointed out, the first foot is often inverted, the stress falling on the first of the two syllables.

Often, however, he deserts the iamb proper for what may best be described as a lilting mixture of iambs, trochees, and anapaests. This is illustrated in the 10.10.11.11. measure, where the lilt is emphasized by the internal rhyme and the extra weak syllable, making a feminine rhyme, in the second couplet, as in 'Ye neighbours and friends of Jesus draw near' (329).

The same mixed rhythm characterizes the stanzas of long and shorter lines, like those of 'Come let us anew' (956) and 'Away with our fears' (278), 'an amazing, magical metre', as Bernard Manning called it. It is, perhaps, at its most effective in the long elaborate stanzas of which 'Worship and thanks and blessing' (412) is a notable example. Mr Findlay points out that Charles Wesley wrote only one hymn ('From trials unexempted',

476) in the familiar 'quiet' iambic eight-lined 7.6. measure; but that his corresponding eight-lined stanza, as in 'Praise the Lord who reigns above' (14), is fundamentally trochaic, making the most of the rhythmic 'hammer blow'. A variant of this stanza is seen in the measure (7.6.7.6.7.8.7.6.) represented by 'Son of God if Thy free grace' (477), which is a lively mixture of iambs and trochees. He also remarks on the strong stresses 'fore and aft' in a measure (6.6.7.7.7.7.), illustrated in 'Jesus, to Thee we fly' (233), which, though a favourite with Wesley himself, has never become a favourite with Methodist congregations, chiefly because it is musically rather unmanageable.

To sum up, then, there is a remarkable freedom in the rhythm and metre of Charles Wesley's hymns. And this is made possible by the fact that he has no inhibitions about rhyme—that is to say, he does not, as far as rhyme is concerned, 'rise to perfection's height'. And in this he is wise. We may safely assume that it was not through carelessness but by a happy intuition that he allowed himself a certain rhyming flexibility. It is part of his experimentalism that, writing as he was for singing, he instinctively introduced a freedom into the 'correctness' of rhyming as well as the metre that characterized the age. Later on, the Romantics—notably Keats and Shelley—availed themselves of the same freedom; and it may even be said that he points the way forward, though he himself would be horrified at the thought, to the echoic devices and assonances of today.

It is important to remember this, because writers on hymnology, especially those who affect a 'literary' attitude, are apt to condemn out of hand the imperfect rhyming in the hymns of Wesley and others. Sometimes they may be justified; but never (or rarely) with Wesley. For this reason it is profitable to make a fairly detailed analysis of the 'imperfect' rhymes in the Wesley hymns, reminding ourselves of exactly what liberties he permits himself, and judging of their effectiveness.

LANGUAGE, METRE, RHYME OF HYMNS

1. Charles Wesley naturally uses 'eye-rhymes', that is, rhymes which are perfect to the eye but not to the ear, like *quay—day*. Here are a few examples out of many: *come—home* (88); *one—Throne* (17); *gone—alone* (68); *have—save* (110, 153); *move—love* (39, 49); *sword—Word* (68); *worth—forth* (96); *are—declare* (49), *spare* (59); *beneath—breath* (14, 304). Such rhymes have always been conventionally accepted by poets. The example given in the first sentence of this note (*quay—day*) is used, for example, by so fastidious a rhymer as Tennyson.

2. He often rhymes associated vowel sounds that differ, however, in the qualities of 'openness' or length. Simple examples are: *sin—clean* (1, 269); *live—receive* (39, 88, 141); *still—feel* (49); *sit—repeat* (350), *feet* (96), *submit* (247); *returned—mourned* (294, 347, 348, 349). Often the discrepancy in the vowel sounds is more marked, as *hell—fail* (246), *seal* (204); *arrayed—glad* (243); *man—contain* (134); *load—blood* (294); *come—womb* (117), *gloom* (349); *blessed—increased* (262); *trust—boast* (343); *fled—made* (39); *claim—am* (188); *up—hope* (87, 200), *droop* (97, 246). There are many others. Sometimes a particular word presents special rhyming difficulties, and Wesley does not hesitate to take liberties. Examples are *God* and *peace*. For *God* he has the rhymes *abroad* (1, 18), *loud* (14), *showed* (39, 142),[1] *blood* (87), *abode* (277), *renewed* (219), and *load* (200, 347); for *peace* he has *holiness* (87), *righteousness* (117), *possess* (275), *confess* (262), as well as *is* (98) and *ease* (319), in which the consonantal correspondence is also imperfect (see paragraph 3 below). For this there is technically, little excuse or defence; but we may well imagine how a too great devotion to technical correctness would have restricted the natural freedom and flow of his language. Moreover, it may well be that some of the discrepancies illustrated were not, in fact, so great in eighteenth-century pronunciation. It is Watts, writing some thirty years before, who tells us that *first* is pronounced (as it still is in some rustic dialects) *fust*,

[1] See note on p. 23.

82 THE WESLEYS AND THE ENGLISH LANGUAGE

and illustrates the point in one of his own hymns:

> *We sing Thine everlasting Son*
> *Who joined our nature to his own*
> *Adam the second from the dust*
> *Raises the ruins of the first.*

3. In all but two of the examples given in paragraph 2 the consonantal correspondence is impeccable. But here, too, Wesley sometimes took liberties, especially with *s* unvoiced or 'sharp' and voiced (=z). This is clearly exemplified in the two rhymes for *peace* given above, and in his rhymes for *praise—grace* (1, 7, 17), *race* (7), *place* (17), and *face* (66). He also has the rhymes *grace—displays* (1), *ways* (96); *face—gaze* (114); *cause—Cross* (75); and *voice—joys* (280). But *peace*, *grace*, and *praise* are such characteristic 'key' words of Wesley, that it is easy to see how impoverished he would have been without this juggling with the *s* sounds.

4. It is well established that in the eighteenth century the *oi* sound before *n*, as in *join*, was pronounced like the long open *i*, as in *wine;* that *e* before *r* was pronounced like the open *a* (*convert, convart*), as it still is in *clerk* and certain other words; and that *ea* was like a long closed *a* in certain words where it is now pronounced *ee*, as in *speak*. To this the rhyming of Pope, Swift, and others amply testifies. In fact, the change to the modern pronunciation of such words was taking place in Wesley's time. He rhymes *join* with *Thine* (17), *divine* (17, 37), *combine* (246), and *joined* with *mankind* (114); *convert* with *heart* (200, 346, 348), and *exert* with *part* (248, 269); and *breaks* with *speaks* (92). For these rhymes, since they were perfect in his time, he needs no defence.

5. He sometimes rhymes a normally unstressed syllable containing the neutral vowel sound represented by the phonetic symbol ə (as in fath*er*) with a stressed syllable containing a more or less associated vowel sound. This is best illustrated in a little group of Whitsun hymns in which he requires the word *Comforter* at the end of a line. Thus

LANGUAGE, METRE, RHYME OF HYMNS 83

the last syllable (*-er*) of *Comforter* rhymes with *here* in 275, with *hear* in 280, with *prayer* in 277, and with *appear* in 349. Similarly, in 306 he rhymes Interpret*er* with *hear* and worshi*ppers* with *bears* in 264. In this category come his rhymes with his favourite words in *-able* and *-ible*, already noticed (pp. 77-8). Though in such words the last syllable is manifestly unstressed, he could not resist sometimes giving them pride of place at the end of a line, and a kind of artificial stress for rhyme's sake. His favourite among them is *unspeakable*, which in 39 and 77 he rhymes with *tell*, in 98 with *hell*, and in 745 with *feel*. We may also notice, though it is not quite in the same class, the rhyme *supply—liberty* (98), where an unstressed is rhymed with a stressed syllable. The remarkable thing is that, though such rhyming does violence to the rhythmical pattern of the verse, it does not offend the ear, at any rate in singing.

6. A special note must be made of his double or 'feminine' rhymes, which are characteristic of his more rollicking measures, including the 10.10.11.11. stanza, where in the last two lines, as already explained, they occur internally. First, we may easily forgive the slight imperfections of *given—heaven* (17 and *passim*), *deliver—ever* (242), and *spirit —merit* (242). But like other poets, he experienced difficulty with feminine rhymes, and took more liberties than usual with them. He uses, for example, *passion—exaltation* (264), *compassion—salvation* (329), *saviour—favour* (251, 420), and, less defensible, *adore Thee—glory* (351, 264), *burdened—pardoned* (329), *venture—enter* (329), *Stephen— heaven* (411). In one familiar hymn (420) he startles, and rather offends, our ears with the rhymes *walk in—talking* and *wearing—appear in*. Perhaps, however, we have here a reminder of the eighteenth century habit of dropping a final *g* after *n*, as in the familiar phrase 'huntin', shootin', and fishin' '.

Wesley is not, indeed, at his happiest in the 10.10.11.11 stanza, partly because the internal rhymes are apt, as it were, to take charge, and produce a somewhat unpleasing rhythmical lilt—an effect which is emphasized when they are feminine and imperfect. It is noteworthy that in the more elaborate stanza 7.7.4.4.7.D, as in 251, 411, 412, the first and sixth lines, which have feminine endings (stressed followed by unstressed) are not rhymed, though we should expect them to be. No doubt instinct told him that two feminine rhymes in a stanza (even a long one) were enough. The compilers of our present hymn-book took it upon themselves to cut out an internal rhyme in 311—

> *O let me commend my Saviour to you,*
> *I set to my seal that Jesus is true.*

Here the 1780 text is—

> *The mercy I feel, To others I shew:*
> *I set to my seal That Jesus is true.*

Perhaps they felt that 'shew' did not nowadays rhyme with 'true', and therefore decided to replace the line which contained it with one from another verse, the rest of which they omitted. They probably felt that the loss of an internal rhyme was not very important.

These are the main types of Wesley's imperfect rhymes. My examples are, in fact, taken from the first third of the hymn-book; there are, of course, many others in the remainder, but it is safe to say that they fall into the same types. Two things have to be remembered: first, that, when all is said and done, the proportion of imperfect to perfect rhymes is very small; and second, that Wesley never or rarely fell under the tyranny of rhyme, partly at least because he admitted a flexibility that broke the tyrant's power. In this he is far superior to some established poets, even those who followed him in taking liberties. When, for example, Keats writes

> My heart aches, and a drowsy numbness pains
> My sense as though of hemlock I had drunk,
> Or emptied some dull opiate to the drains
> Some minute past—

LANGUAGE, METRE, RHYME OF HYMNS 85

he has allowed rhyme to drive him into a simile that contains a ludicrous ambiguity. It is true that *drains* may mean *dregs*—the word he really wanted. But the fact remains that, at first reading, the line suggests the kitchen sink. But we should be hard put to it to find a parallel example in Wesley's hymns. Wesley was concerned above all with what he wanted to say, and what he wanted the people to sing—with piety rather than with poetry; and if rhyme was an obstacle, then rhyme had to go; He used it as a servant, but did not submit to it as a master.

Bernard Manning, Dr Flew, and quite recently the Rev. G. H. Findlay have all, in their various ways, dealt with the language of the hymns—their vocabulary, their syntax, and what Mr Findlay calls their 'patterns of words', especially chains of verbs, nouns, or adjectives (Stop, and gaze, and fall, and own—191), various forms of repetition, and chiasmus, that is, the cross-cross effect of

Who sows in tears in joy shall reap,
With grief who seeks with joy shall find.

To this I would only add a note on a special type of repetition, an 'echoing' rather, which has something of the pregnancy of epigram and paradox. Here are four simple examples, each with its own echo of sense and sound, which gives to the line a peculiar quality of tautness and concentration:

Captive leads captivity (277)

Trouble, and wash the troubled heart (347)

Careless through outward cares I go (575)

Servants to Thy servants here (598)

More subtle, and more profound, are

But God with God is man with man (312)

and, finest of all, the magnificent lines on the Advent hymn (134):

*Being's source begins to be
And God Himself is born.*

The paradox, without the repetition, but with the emphasis on contrast, comes out in the lilting and triumphant last line of 66:

For ever beginning what never shall end;

and sometimes the effect of contrast and apparent contradiction resolves itself into a deliberate figure of speech, technically called 'oxymoron', notably in the third stanza of 737:

There are who suffer for Thy *sake,
Enjoy* Thy *glorious infamy,
Esteem* the *scandal* of the cross,
And only seek divine applause.

It may be pointed out, in passing, that this brief passage not only contains a vivid example (romanized in the quotation) of oxymoron,[2] which is a peculiarly 'Classical' figure, but also, in 'There are who . . .' a Latinized syntactical construction, and three words, *esteem*, *scandal*, and *applause*, which have, in varying degrees, their original Classical sense.

One last word—on metaphor. Like most other poets, and for that matter prose-writers, Charles Wesley did not always see his metaphors through, as it were, to the end. There is a notable example of this in the most famous of all his hymns, 'Jesu, Lover of my soul' (110), of which Manning says that 'even in a hymn where Wesley's control of his metaphors is not the tightest, he still is very active with his quiet skill of weaving a pattern in his words'. But, like Shakespeare's, Wesley's metaphors defy pedantry; we are no more conscious of incongruity in that hymn than we are in the passage where Hamlet speaks of taking arms against a sea of troubles. This, after all, is

[2] The classic example is in Tennyson:
  His honour rooted in dishonour stood,
  And faith unfaithful kept him falsely true.

LANGUAGE, METRE, RHYME OF HYMNS 87

merely an example of sublime carelessness. Wesley is far more often consistent in metaphor, sometimes sustaining one image throughout a whole hymn, and thus achieving that architectural effect, of which Manning speaks (*Hymns of Wesley and Watts*). Thus in 610 the familiar and somewhat trite metaphor of the pilgrimage is kept alive and vivid by a skilful variation of verbs: *travel, hasten, move, steer, aspiring,*[3] *run, travel on, return, contending, urge our way*, and so back to *travel* again. In 386 the image of the fire on the altar strengthens and lights up the first three stanzas. It is a minor weakness of this great hymn that he lets his metaphor go somewhat at the end, though he rescues it triumphantly, if a little late, with the word *sacrifice* in the very last line. The metaphor of the refining, rather than the sacramental or sacrificial, fire undergoes a strange transformation in 519. At first the fire is 'affliction's furnace', in which the Christian walks unburned, like Shadrach, Meshach, and Abednego. But in the last stanza it becomes the refiner's fire, in which he is moulded and minted, receiving at the same time the 'stamp of perfect love'.

This image of the mould, the stamp, and the seal is, indeed, a favourite one with Wesley:

> *Where the indubitable seal*
>   *That ascertains the kingdom mine?*
> *The powerful stamp I long to feel,*
>   *The signature of love divine.* (280)
>
> *Mould as Thou wilt Thy passive clay;*
>   *But let me all Thy stamp receive.* (572)
>
> *Love, Thine image, love impart!*
> *Stamp it on our face and heart!* (713)

But I want to end with one of the briefest, as I think it is one of the most beautiful, of all his metaphors. It occurs in a hymn (721) that breathes the very spirit of early

[3] 'Our course we steer' has a smack of the voyage rather than the journey about it, and *aspiring* is a little off the track.

Methodism—its 'society' of men and women, its love-feasts, its class-meetings, its meetings for prayer:

> *Touched by the loadstone of Thy love,*
> *Let all our hearts agree,*
> *And ever toward each other move,*
> *And ever move toward Thee.*

It was, in a sense, a topical image; for the new electric machine had given it a peculiar significance. But the natural picture of the tiny filings moved irresistibly by the mysterious attractive power was lifted up to a spiritual plane. The people called Methodists were drawn together in sacred and mysterious fellowship because they were first irresistibly drawn by the magnet of their Master's love.

www.ingramcontent.com/pod-product-compliance
Lightning Source LLC
Chambersburg PA
CBHW071203090426
42736CB00012B/2431